Botham

Botham

Photographs and captions by Patrick Eagar

Essay by John Arlott
Text by Graeme Wright

The Kingswood Press

Photographs and captions © 1985 by Patrick Eagar
Text copyright © 1985 by Graeme Wright, John Arlott
Statistics copyright © 1985 by Bill Frindall

Published by The Kingswood Press, Kingswood, Tadworth, Surrey
An imprint of William Heinemann Ltd.
Second impression 1985
Typeset by Signal Communications
Reproduced by Imago Publishing Ltd.
Printed in Great Britain by Jolly & Barber Ltd., Rugby, Warwickshire
on Silverblade Art 135 gsm supplied by Link Publishing Papers
Bound in Great Britain by Garden City Press Ltd., Letchworth

0 434 98063 3

To
John Arlott

Contents

IAN BOTHAM
An Appreciation

John Arlott

Early Stages

Ian Botham is an instinctive and exultant winner of cricket matches. Ignore, for the moment, the statistics of his play – remarkable as they are – and consider history. If he never scores another run, takes another wicket nor makes another catch, he must stand at the peak of cricket history. In 1981 he did what no one else has ever done or is ever likely to do. He took up a Test series his country was losing and, reshaping it in those mighty hands, decided it by his own efforts from at least one virtually impossible, and another quite precarious position; performed outstandingly in a third, and took ten wickets in the drawn sixth of a six-match series.

To repeat that feat would be beyond even him. But would it? Ever since his first epic Test performance – against New Zealand at Christchurch in 1978 – people have been saying 'He can never do it again'. His answer has been simply to do it again. His immense gift is to make nonsense of probability. Perhaps he has passed his peak; but it would take several years of complete failure to convince anyone who knows him of that.

During a, so far, short first-class career – of the 11 years since he was 18 – he has already known frustration; but has risen spectacularly above it. Above all, he can face the future relatively relaxed. He has nothing to prove – except, that is, to himself, for he accepts every game as a challenge, every game of anything: whether it is cricket, football or golf. Any sport he plays, even against his infant son, is something his nature urges him to win. Describe him, as some do, as a natural competitor; others might prefer to call him a winner. His competitive need is completely without rancour; the ability to laugh is always near the surface. Playing – especially at cricket, which is part of his nature – is fun; heady fun.

It is a significant ingredient of his playing character that he is not really interested in net practice. Some, like Boycott, for instance, will positively work at a net; perfecting a stroke, eradicating a weakness, or simply soaking up practice for practice sake. Ian Botham, though, uses a net for no more than loosening up if his side is to field (and he to bowl), or to get the feel of the ball if they are to bat. A net is not a challenge; no challenge, no fun.

That fun, perhaps better described as joy, is a major ingredient of the pleasure he gives to spectators. He plays with immense zest; taking as well as giving enjoyment. It is, for that reason, almost sad that it is so often necessary to quote figures; but to fail to do so would be to do him less than justice: for he has broken virtually every all-round record for Test cricket: and he is still only 29.

He is a strong man. His frequent playing weight, which could hardly be described as stripped down, for he needs to refuel, and enjoys his relaxation, is about 15 stones. Yet he carries it buoyantly. He has most of the cricketing strokes but he – like those who watch him – most enjoys his athletically free off and cover driving; with, by way of variety, those fearless and violently spectacular hooks.

He applied himself early to cricket. The gift of natural outswing is part of the luck he is never afraid to admit. Diligent application added his inswinger and control of the yorker; but his own explosive nature incorporated a sheer-strength bouncer of hectic lift, which is frequently as counter-productive as it is, for him, irresistible. He is a 'natural' at slip, his speed of reaction taking him rapidly, though unhurriedly, into position: his hands are monumentally safe. Further from the wicket, speed of thought and pure strength of leg take him quickly to the ball and the opportunity of a run-out gives his cricket a single-minded urgency.

The main constituent of his attraction to those who watch is, though, his immense impact on a match. He is no 'art for art's sake' cricketer; has no time for easy runs or cheap wickets; he is in the game to win it. Sometimes, of course, he is trapped in the mesh of a predestined draw; but never through his fault. It may, indeed, be a comment on his captaincy, which romantics will relish, and pragmatists will not, that he would sooner lose a hard match than draw a quiet one.

It is tempting to attempt to define him; a temptation increased by his own reluctance to talk in adjectives. Many see him as a spontaneous cricketer, but he is not completely that. Importantly – and therein lies much of his strength – he is not blinkered. Too many cricketers, sometimes to their cricketing advantage, but often to their human disadvantage, have given themselves to the game to the exclusion of everything else. Ian Botham, despite his success at it has not.

Indeed, he has found deep satisfaction in many pursuits that take him completely away from it; not simply his football, which worries the cricketing establishment, but golf, badminton, shooting, fishing, flying – he holds a private pilot's licence – knocking his house into shape, and building up a cellar of wine. That separation could not have been more valuable if it had been planned instead of instinctive. It helps him to enjoy his cricket and to concentrate on it when concentration is most needed.

Ian Terence Botham was born on 24 November 1955 at Heswall in Cheshire, where his parents kept a home while his father, Leslie, a Chief Petty Officer in the Fleet Air Arm, was stationed in Northern Ireland. When Leslie Botham retired in 1958, he became a test engineer at Westland Helicopters at Yeovil. Thus Ian grew up in Somerset and still stays there during the cricket season; but he has made his home in an enthusiastically restored old farmhouse at Epworth, on the Isle of Axholme, in what is now called South Humberside.

His deep feeling for Somerset, though, is beyond question. He matured as a games player by trailing round with his father to Westland Second XI matches and making up the number when either side was short. He was desperately keen; constantly active: but, for all his eagerness, he was studious about sport. As quite a young boy he would crawl through the hedge of Yeovil Grammar School playing fields and stand there silently watching; absorbing action and atmosphere.

His immense, precocious talent, exciting for his father as well, was soon confirmed on a critical level. He was hailed into the Somerset youth team by Bill Andrews; and Bert Head, that sage soccer manager of Crystal Palace, rang Botham senior to ask if the boy might sign apprentice forms for them. Father and son discussed it; the financial rewards weighed more than a little but Ian, recalling the debate later, said 'Deep down inside I knew I was a better cricketer; besides [which, surely, must have been decisive] I liked it better.' As soon as he left school, in the spring of 1972 at 16, without parting from Somerset, he joyfully took a job on the Lord's ground staff. That shrewd pro, Len Muncer, reported on 'An outstanding cricketer who does everything his own way'.

At the end of August 1973 he left Lord's and, two days later, played his first match for Somerset First XI, against Sussex at Hove in the John Player League. (He scored two; took no wicket for 22 runs, but made a good catch in the deep.) On the following Sunday, against Surrey at The Oval, he again scored two; but took a wicket – that of Geoff Howarth, lbw to a full toss – before the county season ended.

The summer of 1974 was a fine one for Somerset and for Botham. Fifth in the Championship; second in the John Player League, semi-finalists in the Benson and Hedges and the Gillette Cups; the county acquired the exciting West Indian batsman Viv Richards. For Botham there was the wise encouragement and guidance from Peter Robinson and Ken Palmer; and, above all, from that shrewdest of coaches and master of seam bowling, Tom Cartwright, whose skills quite intrigued the young man. Another who had considerable effect on him was Brian Close. They did not always agree; and they both tended to be explosive in disagreement: but a considerable mutual respect grew up between them.

In that season, Tom Cartwright was twice injured and, consequently, Botham played in 16 Championship matches. Learning voraciously, he scored 400 runs at 17.39 and took 27 wickets at 25.18. His major – indeed resounding – success, though, came in a limited-overs game: the quarter-final of the Benson and Hedges Cup against Hampshire, at Taunton. When Ian Botham went in they were 113 for seven, which instantly became 113 for eight; and Somerset, no genuine batting left, faced almost certain defeat against the Antiguan Andy Roberts, at that time about the fastest bowler in the country. Moseley held on; Botham played controlled strokes full of thought.

At 131, Roberts bowled a steep lifter; Botham tried to hook it, missed. It hit him in the mouth and knocked him over. Struggling to sit upright and streaming blood, he spat out a couple of teeth (he lost two more later) drank some of the water brought out to him, but refused to come off. Blood all over him, but head down and looking perfectly calm, he played through eight more overs; and when Bob Herman began the last over but one – Roberts was to bowl the last – Somerset needed three to win. Botham stopped two balls; played at and missed three; the sixth he hammered through the cover boundary to take his score to 45; and give Somerset a win by one wicket. The crowd ran on to the pitch to salute him: the unknown Ian Botham became a local hero and headline news on every sports page in the country.

Into The First Class

He devoted the winter to building his strength navvying on a building site; at Christmas he became engaged to Kathryn Waller. When the new season came round he was bursting with confident young manhood; but it did not work out as his unfailing optimism had planned. 'Closey' diagnosed the trouble: 'Trying too hard, thinking too hard; he'll be all right with time.' His promise was inescapable; the figures did not support it. Four more matches than in the previous year brought 99 more runs, 31 more wickets; but at poorer averages.

Then, 1976. By the end of that year Ian Botham was 21; married; had established his confidence against Sussex at Hove early in the summer with an innings of 97 in which he hit two sixes and 13 fours and was particularly severe on Tony Greig; starting with a six, he made his first century – 167 not out, with six sixes and 20 fours – against Nottinghamshire; was capped by Somerset. Close had promoted him in the batting order to No. 4 or No. 5 and, over all, at the end of the season, the undeniable quality of his cricket – batting, bowling, and catching – won him a place in the English teams for the first and third of the one-day internationals with West Indies. He achieved little (one and 20; two wickets), but his figures for Somerset – third in the batting with 944 runs at 33.71; and most wickets, 60 at 27.41 – established him as already an appreciable county all-rounder still short of his 21st birthday. Indeed, in all matches – three-day and one-day – he made 1,471 runs and took 101 wickets.

His form was recognised with a Whitbread Trust Scholarship to Australia; but the few grade matches he was given in Melbourne did not satisfy his hunger for cricket. His chief gain from the trip was Frank Tyson's advice, which was later to prove valuable, about bowling on Australian pitches.

First, though, the Australians were to tour England; and in 1977 the fixture list emphasised his opportunity. Early in their tour – 18, 19, 20 May – the Australians went to Bath unbeaten, only to lose to Somerset by seven wickets. Botham, with aggressive innings of 59 and 39 not out, and five wickets, including the first four in the Australian second innings, played himself into the MCC side, captained by Mike Brearley, against the tourists. In that match he lost his temper, bowled several peevish and expensive overs which irked Brearley's tidy mind, and was taken off. He had a poor game (10 not out and 0; three wickets for 74).

Although he was picked in the 14-man squad for the one-day internationals, he did not play in any of them; and was not chosen for either of the first two Tests. In the third, at Trent Bridge, however, he replaced the injured Chris Old. Again under the captaincy of Brearley, he bowled an extremely poor opening spell but then, coming on again, an almost ludicrously flukey wicket – that of Greg Chappell – set him on his way. He took five for 74 in the first innings and his Test career was launched.

A not quite certain choice for Leeds, there he rose to the situation and on a helpful wicket bowled a shatteringly hostile spell of five for 21 in the first innings. Although he did not take a wicket in the second innings of either match that gave him a hand-hold on a Test place; primarily, probably, because England won both matches, and the rubber, to regain the Ashes. During that game at Headingley, however, faithfully wearing his ancient 'lucky' boots he trod on the ball and fractured a metatarsal bone in his left foot. That was the end of the season for him; but he was 'on the boat' for the tour of Pakistan and New Zealand.

In the few matches before England went into the Tests with Pakistan, he did not do enough to win a place in a team which, on those slow spinners' pitches, used only two seam bowlers. In New Zealand, matters were different. The pitches were greener, and he effectively got off his tour 'mark' with a quite brilliant century against Canterbury – coming to his hundred with 4, 4, 6. In the first Test, at Wellington, New Zealand achieved their historic first win over England; but Botham's four wickets for 40 were the cheapest taken for England and, more convincingly, his 19 was, out clear, the highest score in their routed second innings of 64.

Then, at Christchurch, he staked an irrefutable claim to take the place of the Packerised Greig as England's all-rounder with the first of his major Test performances. He followed his first Test century – 103 – with five for 73, 30 not out and three for 38; and, for the first but not the last time, the critics were moved to say 'even he can hardly do as much again'. On the perfect pitch at Auckland he took a hard-working five for 109 (34 overs); made an exemplary 53 when the batting became sluggish; but could not prevent a draw. He was second in both the batting (212 at 53) and the bowling averages (17 at 18.29), with the highest aggregate in both instances.

Back home, and under the recovered Brearley (injured in Pakistan), he assumed considerable stature. Against Pakistan he scored 100 in the first Test. Then, at Lord's, where his second scoring stroke was a six into the Mound Stand, he made a splendid 108 off only 104 balls; and, in the second Pakistani innings, took eight for 34. That was the best analysis ever achieved in a Lord's Test; and he became the first player to score a century and take eight wickets in a single innings of a Test. Again, the chorus rose: 'Surely even he can never do as much again.'

He took four for 59 in the rain-ruined third and last Test; and England took the rubber two-nil. Botham was top of the batting (212 at 70.66) and third in the bowling (13 at 16.07).

In the three Tests of the same summer against New Zealand, all of which England won comfortably, he batted only three times (51 at 17.00) but, after four wickets in the first Test, took a match-winning nine in the second and a decisive 11 in the third to finish far out at the top of the bowling with 24 – twice as many as anyone else – at 14.04.

English cricket (if not so positively as Australian) was going through a bad phase. The Packer operation had estranged many of the public, and there can be no doubt that Botham's striking performances did much to sustain its appeal.

So to Australia, again under Brearley, who became only the second England captain (Sir Leonard Hutton was the other) both to regain and retain the Ashes. Botham, who had injured a wrist shortly before the side left, was bursting with eagerness to play; as soon as he did, he imparted his own brand of fire in the belly, and England won their first major match.

He set no rivers on fire but contributed generously to the magnificent team spirit, especially by his resistance in the crucial fourth Test after Australia had narrowed the gap to two-one. He was third in the batting (291 at 29.10) and he took most wickets, 23 (the same number as Geoff Miller) at 24.65. This was convincing evidence that, even when not in the limelight, he was still an ideal team man, batting, bowling and fielding not only with all his great natural ability, but also with all his heart and strength.

By now some essential facets of Ian Botham's cricketing character had emerged. Perhaps most significantly, Mike Brearley had discovered how to motivate him; sometimes by playing down the extent of a challenge; at others, pulling his leg to rouse him; always ready to put in a word of guidance without dictating. It worked; and, so far as it was ever possible to judge, Botham was utterly happy to play under him.

He had entered into fast-bowling challenges with the Australian Rodney Hogg – with only a bottle of beer at stake, but none the less keen for that – on who should take the other's wicket more often; with Richard Hadlee in a bouncer competition. There was, too, a rivalry – which strongly motivated both of them – with his friend, Viv Richards, based on one outscoring the other; but also, at times, apparently, on whom could play the most extravagant strokes. Brian Rose, Somerset's captain, did his shrewd best to keep the two from such competitive – or self destructive – partnerships by separating them in the batting order.

Since Botham had started to play for Somerset the county had, at first largely coincidentally, done well in the County Championship and had made an increasingly positive mark in the one-day competitions. Test-match calls meant that Botham's county appearances averaged only about 10 – roughly half the first-class fixtures – a season. For four years, though, from 1975 to 1978, he took most wickets for them in Championship matches; and, in 1980, emerged as a more successful batsman, heading their averages with 875 runs at 62.50.

In 1978 Somerset had been, to their bitter disappointment, beaten Gillette Cup finalists and, narrowly, runners-up in the John Player League. In 1979, to immense delight within the county, they won both competitions with Botham always the team man, constantly doing something useful. Yet the Sunday – John Player – matches probably brought him more chagrin than any other cricket he ever played. Somerset have, unhappily, a disturbing posse of drunken oicks who appear sickeningly at all their Sunday matches, barracking and generally distorting the play and the atmosphere. The club ought to take serious steps about that.

He had an indifferent Prudential (World) Cup competition; and there were those to suggest that the constant strain of pace bowling, attacking batting, slip fielding, and world travel were beginning to tell even on his magnificent constitution. After this tournament India, with a strong batting side, the pace of Kapil Dev, and the spin of Bedi, stayed on to play a four-Test rubber which England took as narrowly as one-nil. It was Botham's dismissal of Gavaskar (221), Yashpal Sharma and Yajurvindra Singh in the last innings which barred India from the win which would have drawn the rubber.

Named as Man of the Series, Botham continued to chalk up records. When he had Gavaskar caught at slip by Brearley at Lord's it was his 100th Test wicket, taken in the shortest time – two years nine days from his début – a new record, but one which was beaten by Kapil Dev the following winter. At Leeds he saved the English innings from collapse at 58 for four with an innings of 137 (in a total of 270). After more than two days lost to rain, he began on Monday nine not out; he completed his century with a six off Kapil Dev, in the last over before lunch, hit the next ball for four and then, remembering his captain's feelings, blocked the next four balls, not realising that a single would have given him the first English century before lunch in a Test since 1935. However, Jim Laker, presenting him with the Man of the Match award, described this as 'one of the finest Test innings of the last 20 years'. His first runs, a boundary, in The Oval Test took him to the Test 'double', 1,000 runs and 100 wickets, in the record shortest time of 21 matches.

That winter, it was back to Australia again, for the Benson and Hedges World Series Cup – in which England eliminated Australia by beating them four times. But, despite Botham's three for 33 and resistant 37, they lost both 'finals' to West Indies. During that competition, England also played a three-match rubber in which the Ashes were, specifically, not at stake. Australia, their Packer players returned, won all three matches: Botham scored a century; had 187 runs at 37.40 and was top of the bowling in aggregate and average – 19 at 19.52 (next best, 13 at 31.15).

On the return journey, England played in the Indian Golden Jubilee Test at Bombay and defeated India – previously unbeaten in 15 Tests – by 10 wickets, thanks almost entirely to Botham. Rising above the general fatigue of both sides and seemingly constantly 'in' the match, he took six for 58 in the Indian total of 242; then, after England collapsed to 58 for five, he played a conscientious, sound, but also enterprising innings of 114; picking the ball to hit, he struck 17 fours. Then he proceeded to take seven Indian second-innings wickets for 48. Thus he became the first man to score a century and take 10 or more wickets in a Test. And again, if with decreasing vehemence, the chorus announced 'even he can never do that again'.

Bob Taylor, who stayed with Botham in the decisive – and record sixth-wicket – stand of 171, also set a record with 10 catches in a Test – eight of them from Botham's bowling.

After that, Mike Brearley announced that he would not again be available to captain an overseas tour. It was only fair to give his successor experience in the office; England's captaincy was offered to Ian Botham who, proudly, happily and confidently accepted.

The Unhappy Captaincy

Many a good cricketer could have told how captaincy can affect playing performance, especially that of an all-rounder. Certainly, too, Botham had virtually no experience of the post. Few, though, would have thought that this talented, optimistic, competitive constant winner was about to enter on the least successful phase – one,

indeed, of almost unbroken failure – of his career.

Between 5 June 1980 and 7 July 1981 he took England into 12 Tests which resulted in four defeats and eight draws; to equal their longest sequence up to then without a win. The other was Leeds 1963 to The Oval 1964.

Botham's own figures were equally depressing. Up to his appointment his Test record read:

Matches	Innings	Not Out	Runs	Highest Score	Average	100s	50s
25	35	2	1,336	137	40.48	6	3
Balls	Runs	Wickets	Average	Best Bowling	5 Wkts/ Inns	10 Wkts/ Match	
6,228	2,575	139	18.52	8-34	14	3	

In his 12 matches as captain, the figures were:

Matches	Innings	Not Out	Runs	Highest Score	Average	100s	50s
12	21	0	276	57	13.14	–	1
Balls	Runs	Wickets	Average	Best Bowling	5 Wkts/ Inns	10 Wkts/ Match	
2,211	1,158	35	33.08	4-77	–	–	

All 12 matches, of course, were against the fiercest competition in the world – West Indies (9) and Australia (3). It was, though, a picture of unrelieved gloom for him.

He celebrated the appointment with 228 at Taunton in the county's 'blood' match against Gloucestershire at Whitsun. In the two one-day internationals against West Indies, England batted too slowly in the first, but Botham, with 42 not out, saw them safely home in the second by three wickets.

In the first innings of the first Test he made 57. That was his highest score as captain. From then on nothing went right for Ian Botham. West Indies won the series by the only Test finished; but they had the better of the four draws. The Centenary Test with Australia at Lord's, at the end of the season, was a bitter match for him. Australia had the better of it; there were unpleasant scenes when the crowd, not without some justification, objected to the amount of time sacrificed after rain. At the end, when Greg Chappell set England 370 to win in 350 minutes, the English batsmen, presumably acting on uncharacteristic orders from their captain, made no attempt to get them. What had been planned as a celebration ended in general disenchantment.

The winter tour to West Indies was a grim follow-up. West Indies won two-nil; Botham's top score was 26, and though he finished top of the bowling (15 at 32.80) he was no match-winner. The cancellation of the Georgetown Test in protest against the presence of Robin Jackman, who had been playing in South Africa, and the death of the well-liked assistant-manager, Ken Barrington, seemed to emphasise the disappearance of Botham's luck.

Once back to face the Australians, England were well

beaten at Nottingham. In the Lord's Test, played in a bad crowd-atmosphere, Botham for the first time suffered a 'pair' in a Test: the result was an unhappy draw; and at the end Botham resigned the captaincy.

The press had been giving him a bad time and now the crowds gave him little sympathy. Just as his good fortune had been so glorious before the appointment, now all had gone correspondingly sour. The bounce had gone out of his stride. Even he, in his natural optimism, could not dream that his greatest triumphs lay only days ahead.

The Great Days

When he announced his resignation – probably anticipating the selectors' decision – Botham said he hoped Mike Brearley would take over; and so it was. The new captain returned to Test cricket at Leeds, a ground where he had rarely been at all happy (two Test ducks and one in a one-day). Fortunately he is not superstitious.

When Brearley and Botham met for the first time since he took over the captaincy, he commiserated with him on the embarrassment he had suffered; then, at once, 'Do you want to play or be left out, Both?' It was at once a considerate and a challenging remark; indicative of his understanding of his man. 'Left out? Me? Not bloody likely!' Importantly for both of them, that was now settled.

Incidentally, although the family pronounce the 'both' syllable of the name like that word, he is generally known in the dressing-room as 'Both' with the o pronounced as in 'not'.

Initially there had been a suggestion that Botham should be 'rested' to rediscover his confidence. He himself had an idea that if Mike Brearley had not been appointed he – Botham – might not have played. There was an even stronger possibility that Bob Willis would be left out. He had bowled 32 no-balls at Lord's; and afterwards taken to his bed with a chest infection. Only after Bernard Thomas, the physiotherapist, declared him fully fit was Willis – providentially as it proved – included in the side.

Kim Hughes won the toss; Australia batted on a dull, cloudy day and were 203 for three at the end of it. Botham took Wood's wicket; but dropped Dyson, who went on to score 102, and Trevor Chappell. Brearley tended to use Botham in short, three- or four-over spells in order, he reasoned, to keep him eager to bowl.

Surely enough the psychological ploy worked. On the second day Botham came to him and said 'Give me a good long spell, skip, and I'll get you some wickets'. He was as good as – or better than – his word. All of a sudden he looked like his old self; the ball began to move and bounce. In his after-tea spell he took five wickets for 35; six altogether, for 95; the first time he had mustered as

many as five in a Test innings since he had taken over the captaincy.

Boycott and Gooch saw the day out without event; that was reserved for Saturday, when Lillee, Alderman and Lawson moved the ball about freakishly. Only Botham, hitting out boldly, made more than 24; his 50 was brave and chanceless in an England innings which subsided abjectly to 174. Hughes asked England to follow on and Gooch went that night before a run was scored. On Monday the same three bowlers, especially Alderman, chopped England down equally savagely to 135 for seven before Dilley came in to Botham with England needing 92 to avoid an innings defeat. The players and all the 'circus' booked out of their hotels and waited for another four-day defeat for England.

The two, with little to hope for, began to bat freely, hitting and missing but never edging fatally: growing in confidence as none of the other batsmen had. They put on 117 in little over the hour before Dilley played on to Alderman. Old, following him, helped with another 67; and, when the last man, Willis, was out next morning, England had reached 356. Botham 149, had rarely batted better, more determinedly or more valuably. He reached his hundred off only 87 balls. He became, too, only the second man – the Australian, J.M. Gregory was the first – to score a century and take five wickets in an innings in an Anglo-Australian Test. In all his Test cricket he had now done that four times; twice more than anyone else.

The innings defeat had been avoided; but Australia needed only 130 to win. Botham had Wood caught by Taylor at 13, but, at 56 for one, Australia were cruising home when Willis changed ends and, quite simply, bowled them out. Nine wickets fell for 55 runs; Willis, in the finest performance of his Test career, took eight for 43, finishing it all off with a yorker which removed Bright's middle stump. England, not simply against the odds, but to the amazement of all – including themselves – had won by 18 runs. It was only the second time that a side had won a Test after following on.

It is difficult to escape the conclusion that, from that day on, for the rest of the series, Australia were uneasily, almost superstitiously, fearful that England, and especially Botham, might yet again perform the virtually impossible. He, for his part, went to Edgbaston twice the man he had been a fortnight before; and buoyant with another success. On the Saturday between the third and fourth Tests, Somerset had beaten Surrey in the final of the Benson and Hedges Cup; with a useful conclusive innings by Botham.

At Birmingham though, he could not roll out the big score. The pitch was dry and unreliable, producing the occasional squatter. In England's rather ramshackle first innings, his responsible, for him somewhat careful, 26 was second highest to Brearley's 48, which in the event proved the top score of the match; but a total of 189 fell far short of command.

Wood and the Australian middle order all looked briefly secure: Botham had Bright lbw with a bouncer which 'didn't', but 44 extras contributed largely to Australia's lead of 69, which was enough to look healthy on such a pitch. It looked even better when Bright first tied down and then broke open the England second innings and Alderman finished it off for 219. Even that was largely due to Gatting and Emburey, who put on 39 for the seventh wicket, and Emburey and Taylor, 50 for the ninth. Australia were left needing a bare 151, the lowest innings of the match, to win.

Wood was lbw to Old on that third (Saturday) evening and when Willis removed Dyson and Hughes on Sunday it became 29 for three. Border and Yallop gritted away to 62 for three by lunch; England had kept them to 53 off 30 overs; but wickets were a desperate need. Emburey was making the ball turn and at 105 – only 46 wanted – Brearley was about to bring on his other off-spinner, Willey; Botham agreed with the move. Then, suddenly, Emburey made one not simply turn but lift freakishly and it bounced off Border's glove to Gatting at short leg. On the spur of the moment Brearley turned to Botham. 'Keep it tight for Emburey', he said.

Botham did more than that. He abandoned the twitchy turn that had crept into his run-up over the past year and here he was, coming in, as of old, straight and solid, like some great shire horse, the bounce back in his stride. The conditions did not favour swing and he was bowling at his old fastest. Bright, for instance, was beaten by speed alone.

Crowd feeling rose to an incredulous, feverish delight as, in the next 40 minutes – just 28 balls – he took the remaining five Australian wickets for one run. England had won by a more than improbable 29 runs. Botham had again staggered the Australians and, for the second time in the series, was made Man of the Match; though some thought Emburey had deserved it for making Botham's final stroke possible. Botham himself was gloriously and exuberantly delighted.

So England went to Old Trafford two-one up in the series: and Brearley took first innings. Again the batting was uncertain. Only Tavaré, brought in for the first time in the series, Gatting and, surprisingly at the end, Allott gained any credit in a total of 231 (Botham 0). But Australia's reply must have disappointed them. On a perfectly true pitch, Willis (four for 63) and Botham (three for 28) put them out for 130 to give England a totally unexpected lead of 101. Equally unexpected was the early second-innings collapse. Only Tavaré held as Alderman, rising to the occasion again, reduced them to 104 for five.

That made England's lead 205, which – on the assumption that Australia could not fail a second time on such a well-made and easy pitch – was not enough. So again Botham came in to a difficult position. As he explained afterwards; at Headingley, where England had no logical chance, he could ride his luck with a clear conscience: any runs would be a bonus. Here the problem was one of consolidation, and he was acutely conscious that the new ball was soon due. He played himself in carefully; three singles from his first 30 balls. In his first hour he received 59 balls off which he scored 28 runs. Then Alderman and Lillee took the new ball; which, true to his character, sent Botham's adrenalin pumping. When Lillee bowled bouncers at his head he hooked him for three sixes in two overs. Twice he looked down the line and hooked so imperiously as to take the ball off his eyebrows and send it 30 yards beyond the two long-leg fieldsmen. Once, too, he drove Lillee back, head high, so fiercely that the bowler ducked away; 22 off one over. A marginally short ball from Alderman was pulled hugely over mid-wicket for another six.

At Headingley, because of the uncertainty of the pitch, there were edges, misses and misjudgements. Here there were not. It was a quite princely innings; of style, poise, certainty and immense power. Those two eyebrow sixes off Lillee, perfectly caught by the television camera, remain unforgettably imprinted on the eye of memory. From the time the new ball was taken, when he was at 28, he reached his century – with a sweep for six off Bright – in only 27 more balls. Indeed, it was made off one ball less than at Headingley. To his surprise, his six sixes set a new record for a Test in England, or any against Australia.

So Australia needed 506 to win; or to bat 10 hours for a draw. Two wickets fell early and cheaply before Hughes and, more prolifically, Yallop and Border mounted a stern resistance; it was a question of chipping away. All four main bowlers – Willis, Allott, Botham and Emburey – did their share, Botham with two wickets (for 86) and a fine high slip catch. Australia were all out 402; England had won the fifth Test by 103 runs; and according to English reckoning retained the Ashes; by Australian calculations, regained them; but won them anyway.

Since he stepped down from the captaincy, Ian Botham had played in, and effectively won, three Test matches – and a rubber – with 346 runs at 69.20 and 18 wickets at 16.55. There is not a remotely parallel performance in Test history; not only was it statistically an amazing feat; it was so handsomely executed. And on the following Sunday, for Somerset against Hampshire, he scored a century in only 67 minutes – the second fifty in nine minutes – in the course of a stand of 179 with his friendly rival, Viv Richards: a record for the fifth wicket in the competition.

It had been a hard year, from the series in West Indies

through that with Australia, and its casualties were to be counted when the England side was chosen for the sixth Test at The Oval. Of the basic Test eleven in West Indies, only John Emburey, Geoffrey Boycott and Ian Botham remained. If ever there were evidence of Botham's stamina and durability, this was it. The rubber was decided; but The Oval match, although it was drawn, was an absorbing one.

Brearley put Australia in but, by the second morning, England were in some disarray. Of the three pace bowlers, Hendrick had a strained rib muscle, Willis pulled stomach muscles, and Botham a damaged left knee and a trapped nerve in his back. None of them could bowl flat out. Australia made 352 (Border 106 not out): England replied with 314 (Boycott 137); and Australia, declaring at 344 for nine (Wellham 103, on his début, Border 84), set them 383 to win. Gatting 56, Brearley 51 and Knott 70 not out gave them a draw at 261 for seven. Botham, without fireworks but by solid, medium-pace graft, and in agony every time his left foot hit the ground, bowled 89 overs to take 10 for 253. That gave him 34 wickets; more than any other English bowler; at 20.58 in the series. Those figures took him, too, to his 200th wicket in his 41st Test, in the record time of four years 34 days; and he became the youngest man, at 25 years 280 days, to do so. Overall, his cricket – and hence England's results – in 1981 did more for the image of English cricket than any single facet of the game for many years.

Man of Cricket History

Now the chorus of 'Even he . . .' was hushed. If he had reached a high peak, he still continued to make history. In India during the following winter, in a grim – and for England a losing – series (of the six Tests, five were drawn) Botham batted with conscientious steadiness; was top of the batting (440 at 55.00) and took most wickets (17 at 38.82). He also became the third player – Richie Benaud and Garfield Sobers were the others – to complete the double of 2,000 runs and 200 wickets in Tests. Significantly, too, he did so in fewest matches – 42; the shortest time – four years 126 days; and at the (then) lowest age – 25 years 280 days.

In 1982, England narrowly beat the visiting sides from India and Pakistan. Against the Indians, Botham scored 128 at Old Trafford and 208 at The Oval. His 200, with four sixes and 19 fours, came off 220 balls in 268 minutes. In time it was the third-fastest Test double-century for England; but Bill Frindall believes that, calculated by balls received, it may have been the fastest in all Test cricket. His aggregate of 403 runs (at 134.33) set a new record for England against India in England.

He made 163 (at 27.16) in the generally low-scoring rubber against Pakistan; but with 18 (at 26.55) took eight more wickets than any other Englishman, including six – and the first two batsmen of each innings – in the first Test; and nine in the third. These were the two which England decisively won.

He had, for him, a relatively undistinguished tour of Australia in 1982-83, when he scored only 270 runs (at 27.00); but he and Willis took most wickets, 18 (Botham's at 40.50). When, crucially, he had Thomson caught by Miller at Melbourne, to give England their only win in the series, as narrowly as by three runs, it was his hundredth Test wicket against Australia. It completed his double of 1,000 runs and 100 wickets against them. He was the fourth man to do that in Anglo-Australian Tests; and contrived it in fewer Tests, 22, than any of the other three: Wilfred Rhodes (37) and the Australians M.A. Noble (29) and George Giffen (30).

At last, in 1983, signs of fatigue began to show through even his great strength from too much – and, more important, too intensive – cricket. He scored a century against New Zealand at Trent Bridge – off 99 balls, the second fifty off 26 – when he also struck 26 off two overs from his old rival, Richard Hadlee, with the new ball.

Benefiting from the rest after the domestic season, he began the tour of Fiji, New Zealand and Pakistan at Wellington with a century and five wickets in an innings for the fifth time in Tests: no one else has done it more than twice. He was third in the batting with 226 at 56.50; but his seven wickets cost 50.57. And after the first innings of the first Test in Pakistan he had to return home with, apparently, a recurrence of his old knee injury.

It was a disappointing tour for England, too. They lost their three-match rubbers in each country in a single game. The press made play with lurid reports of drug-taking parties among the players. Botham sued one of the papers concerned.

Back in England to face West Indies, Botham also took over the captaincy of Somerset. In a one-sided series, West Indies won all five Tests by substantial margins; but Botham offered the sturdiest resistance. He was second in the batting with 347 runs at 34.70; and he took most wickets, 19 at 35.10 including an heroic eight for 103 at Lord's and five for 72 at The Oval.

When he had Dujon caught at first slip in the latter match – his 72nd Test – he became the fifth bowler to take 300 wickets in Tests; the first – and, surely, for long the only – man to perform the 'triple double' of 3,000 runs and 300 wickets in Tests. Then, in the single Test against Sri Lanka at Lord's he equalled S.F. Barnes's world record by taking five or more wickets in a Test for the 24th time.

Replacing Brian Rose as captain of Somerset – a promotion which he must have regarded with a streak of anxiety through even his habitual optimism – he had a good year.

The side was considerably weakened by the absence of Viv Richards and Joel Garner with the touring West Indians, and of Botham himself at the Tests, and it was, despite the reinforcement of the New Zealander, Martin Crowe, a good performance to reach the quarter-finals of the NatWest and Benson and Hedges Cups; and, most important, to climb three places to seventh in the County Championship.

He wisely decided not to make , with England, the tours of India and the one-day tournament in Australia in favour of a winter at home with his family. But in the New Year it was announced that police raiding Ian Botham's house had found a small quantity – about two smokes – of cannabis there. He was charged with its possession. He said it had been given to him some time before during a West Indian party, and there was no reason to doubt his word: but he was fined. Several people wrote to say they could give a good guess as to who had tipped off the police. Shortly after it was reported that some police forces habitually did no more than caution first offenders found in possession of 'grass': and that several chief constables regarded it as so unimportant by comparison with the 'big' drugs that they favoured making its possession legal.

Botham's performances have often recalled the story of George Hirst after he had performed the double of 2,000 runs and 200 wickets in an English season. Someone asked him if he thought anyone else would ever do it? 'Ah doan't knaw', he answered, 'but ah'll tell thi summat; if he does he'll be bloody tired.'

The dual labour of batting and pace bowling, coupled with close fielding at Test level, imposes a cruel strain. Only five other cricketers have discharged it to measurable extent; Walter Hammond, Keith Miller, Kapil Dev, Richard Hadlee, and Imran Khan. It is illuminating to compare their records.

It is beyond all doubt that Ian Botham has cricketing greatness in him; perhaps to a greater extent than anyone else in the whole history of the game. He has fired the imagination of cricket followers to a striking degree; and showed the chorus that, despite their doubts, he could go on doing it.

He emerged from a winter of trial and the kind of rest which he all too soon finds irksome, without as some of his friends feared – exploding. He began at once to bat in his most dramatic fashion. His bowling was not instantly of his highest standard but, then, he is one of those bowlers – Derek Shackleton was another – who bowled themselves fit. Of the batting there could be no doubt; on his 'day' he was magnificent. 'Day' tended at first to be the operative word. At Taunton he savaged Border's Australian bowlers with 50 off 30 balls in the evening. Hampshire came in for a more sustained mauling. Then, in the

BATTING

	M	I	NO	HS	R	Avge	100s	50s	Catches
W.R. Hammond	85	140	16	336*	7,249	58.45	22	24	110
K.R. Miller	55	87	7	147	2,958	36.97	7	13	38
Kapil Dev	68	101	9	126*	2,788	30.30	3	15	26
Imran Khan	51	77	12	123	2,033	31.12	2	7	16
R.J. Hadlee	57	96	12	103	2,088	24.85	1	10	29
I.T. Botham	**73**	**117**	**3**	**208**	**4,159**	**36.48**	**13**	**18**	**84**

BOWLING

	Balls	Runs	Wkts	Avge	Best	5WI	10Wm
W.R. Hammond	7,967	3,138	83	37.80	5-36	2	–
K.R. Miller	10,461	3,906	170	36.97	7-60	7	1
Kapil Dev	14,523	7,406	258	28.70	9-83	18	2
Imran Khan	12,551	5.316	232	22.91	8-58	16	4
R.J. Hadlee	14,292	6,341	266	23.85	7-23	19	4
I.T. Botham	**16,881**	**8,191**	**312**	**26.25**	**8-34**	**24**	**4**

Figures correct to May 1985

one-day internationals he bowled tidily and responsibly if not at his peak. On the other hand, he batted more convincingly than he has usually done in the over-limit game. At a time when he looked likely to win the match he was out playing the reverse sweep, a stroke which the Chairman of Selectors forthwith proscribed. Although Mike Gatting might disagree, it is an impossible stroke. To 'blame' Botham for it, though, is to criticize adversely all he has ever done which seemed impossible but which ultimately proved almost miraculously successful.

If, though, he were never to appear in another match, we should remember Ian Botham as a colossus in the cricket field who played that game with such skill, power and gusto as to leave all of us who follow it for ever indebted to him.

MAY 1985

1

Star Quality

'He glowed with good humour and glorious batting adventure, his broad grin belying the withering force of his exquisitely timed strokes. His happy desire to hit the ball, of course, got him out often when he should have built a big innings.'

So wrote *Wisden* of a Somerset newcomer in 1974. A decade later, those words could be used again to describe Ian Botham, for the good humour, the sense of adventure and that happy desire to hit the ball have become the hallmark of his cricket. They are what make crowds hum with anticipation as, arms awhirl, he makes his way from the pavilion to the middle. But while appropriate now, they were not written about Ian Terence Botham: they belong to Isaac Vivian Richards, Botham's great friend and yet, paradoxically, something of a burden also.

These two great cricketers made their first-class débuts for Somerset against Lancashire in 1974. The 22-year-old Richards scored 1,200 runs in the season and that winter played in his first Test match for West Indies: the 18-year-old Botham, whose first appearances for the county had come at the end of 1973 in two John Player League games, enjoyed a promising season, highlighted by his triumph in Somerset's quarter-final victory over Hampshire in the Benson and Hedges Cup. 'Botham also showed star quali-

ty' said *Wisden*, and portraits of the pair headed the review of Somerset's season.

Rarely, though, have their two talents fused simultaneously for Somerset. The younger Botham, while appreciating Richards's genius, regarded him also as a challenge: someone whose style and performance he had to better. And too often, in trying to out-Viv his teammate, he managed no more than an imitation of the West Indian's hubris. In such circumstances it is usually the team that suffers most.

Statistically, of course, there is no longer any reason for their rivalry, for while Richards is among the leading batsmen of his time, Botham is *the* outstanding all-rounder of his age. In Test cricket only his schoolboy idol, Gary Sobers, stands ahead of him. 'A very outstanding cricketer who shows a great deal of promise but does everything his own way. He needs a lot of guidance . . .' was the shrewd assessment of the coaching staff when Ian was on the Lord's ground staff in 1972 and 1973. And prophetically: '. . . in the course of time will prove to be a more than useful bowler.'

At Taunton, on his return from Lord's, Somerset's elders set about developing the bowling Botham. 'His action is extraordinarily reminiscent of the master's', wrote one cricket journalist in 1975, comparing him to the former England and Warwickshire seam bowler, Tom Cartwright, who had moved to Somerset in 1970. He went into his delivery stride from a good sideways-on approach, had a high action in which the body rather than the arm did the work, and he could swing the ball either way, getting his natural outswinger to leave the bat late.

It was pace, however, as well as movement which did Barry Richards in the 1974 Benson and Hedges quarter-final at Taunton, dismissing Hampshire's master batsman for 13 as Somerset claimed four wickets in 12 balls. Hampshire eventually set Somerset a target of 183 from their 55 overs, but at 113 for seven, with Botham and the tailenders Moseley and Clapp to come, the West Country supporters had been reduced to silence. Immediately upon Botham's arrival it became 113 for eight as Cartwright skyed a catch to deep mid-on.

Of the 70 runs Somerset required for victory, Botham scored 45. At first his partner, Moseley, defended while Ian set about the bowling, and their first five overs together brought 20 runs, including a massive hook by Ian that cleared the ground. Then Gilliat, Hampshire's captain, recalled his strike bowler Andy Roberts, an Antiguan (like Viv Richards) playing his first Championship season after cutting a swathe through county Second XIs the previous year. 'How many?' Desmond Eagar, the Hampshire secretary, would ask when the Seconds returned to Southampton – and it was difficult to know if he meant Roberts's body count or the wickets he had taken.

Now Botham was to be his next victim, beaten by the fearsome pace and bounce as he bravely attempted to hook a short ball. It thwacked into the side of his face, breaking two teeth and jarring loose two more on the other side of his jaw. 'I didn't feel the pain until the next day', Ian was to say later, and if anything the blow served to make his batting more determined. The fastest bowler around was not going to get the better of him! The yorker that followed the bouncer was struck for three, later there was another six, and when Roberts finally trapped Moseley lbw, Somerset required seven runs with more than two overs remaining.

A leg-bye first ball got Clapp (highest score 1 not out) away from Roberts, and Ian defended till the last ball. One run would have sufficed to give Ian the strike but ambitiously they went for three. Clapp, from a long way out, stretched all of his six feet four inches to beat the return. Three times in Herman's last over Ian played and missed; twice he left well alone. The sixth delivery he put foot and bat to the pitch of the ball and it creamed across the cover field for four: the winning boundary. 'Botham received the Gold Award and was wildly cheered . . .' was how *Wisden* understated the pandemonium which followed as the new hero was engulfed by jubilant, unbelieving supporters.

A month later Ian hit his maiden first-class fifty (59 v Middlesex, including two sixes and seven fours) and in August, against Lancashire, he took five wickets in an innings for the first time. In first-class matches that season he finished with 441 runs and 30 wickets, in 1975, a season of consolidation, he had 584 runs and 62 wickets, the most by any Somerset bowler. His fielding, anywhere, was magnificent, a feature of every appearance.

It was in 1976 that Ian at last began to realise his potential as a batsman. Batting higher up the order he essayed his formidable strokeplay in the most exciting fashion, and at Trent Bridge came his maiden century in what were typical Botham circumstances. Nottinghamshire, set up initially by a Derek Randall double-century, had asked Somerset to chase 301 in 230 minutes; and Ian, who had scored a sparkling 80 in the first innings, swept them to victory with seven overs to spare, hitting six sixes and 20 fours in his unbeaten 167. That season he passed 1,000 runs and took 66 wickets, including match figures of 11 for 150 (6 for 25, 5 for 125) against Gloucestershire at Taunton. Bowling 37 overs in the second innings, he was already proving, at 20, that it was impossible to keep him out of the game.

In late August, after the Test series, England's selectors included Ian in their squad for the Prudential Trophy one-day matches against the victorious West Indians. In the first match, dominated by Vivian Richards's 119 not out, Ian's three overs cost 26 runs for the wicket of Lawrence Rowe; in his second (the third of the series) he scored 20 and his three overs cost 30 runs – six coming when Gordon Greenidge hit him clear out of the Edgbaston ground. It was a mean baptism for the young all-rounder.

Although he had played in 1973, one of Ian Botham's first games for Somerset was a Benson and Hedges match against Hampshire at Taunton. A remarkable day for the 18 year old began in the morning session when he bowled the prolific Barry Richards for 13 (top and left). He took one more wicket, that of Peter Sainsbury, during his 11 over spell.

He came in to bat after a collapse had Somerset 113 for seven in reply to Hampshire's 182. It wasn't long before a bouncer from Andy Roberts had hit Botham in the mouth, loosening teeth (right); Sainsbury checks the damage (far right).

In one-day tradition, excitement mounted with many near run outs (top).

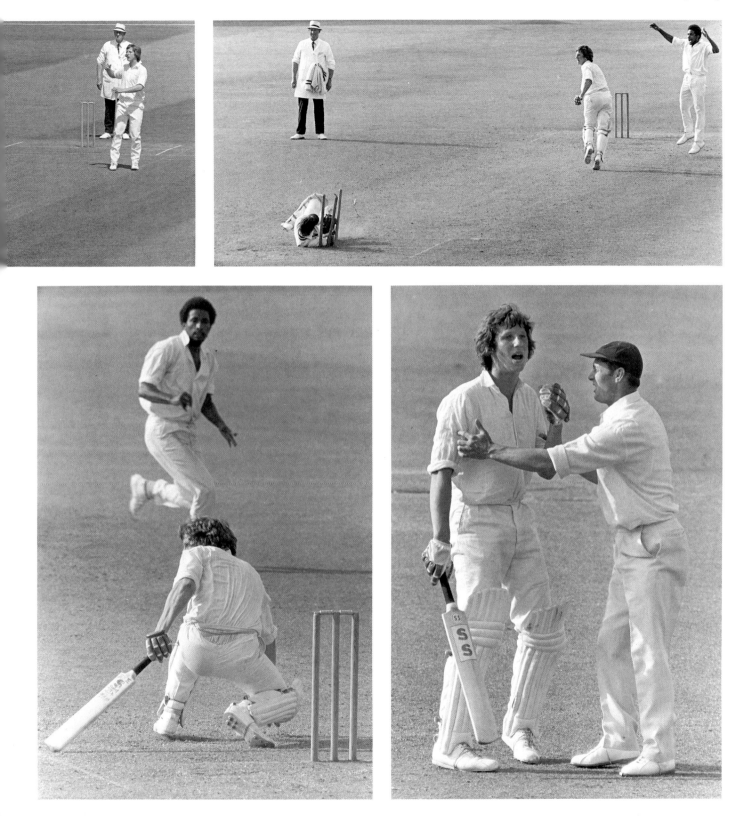

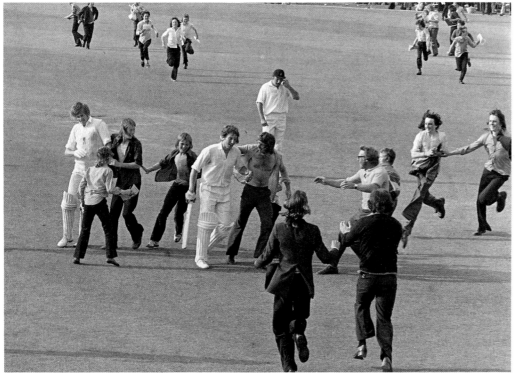

In an extraordinary display of determination and aggression Botham scored 45 runs to win the match and the adoration of all Somerset.

Botham's 1974 season had other highlights, though none could match his performance against Hampshire. He bowled Colin Cowdrey for 8 in the Gillette Cup semi-final (below).

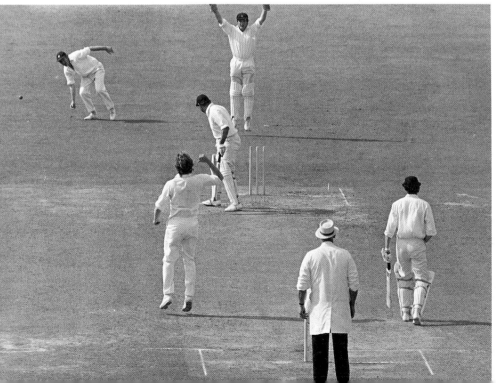

Kent won that match at Canterbury, although Botham scored 19 (above). He shares in a celebration with Viv Richards (right) after the latter had caught Denness on the boundary.

Botham progressed in 1975, and is seen batting against Hampshire again (left and opposite, top left).

The 1976 season found him representing his country for the first time – against the all-powerful West Indies in the one-day Prudential Trophy matches which games followed the Test series. In the third of these at Edgbaston, he made a creditable 20 (opposite top centre and right).

The following year Ian was picked for MCC to play against the Australians at Lord's – made 10 and 0 and took three wickets (right).

The Australians were beaten by Somerset at Bath two games before the MCC match at Lord's. These two photographs were taken during the opening spell in which Ian Botham took the first four Australian wickets to fall in the second innings. It was a bowling action the Australians were to become familiar with by the end of the summer.

2

Test Player

The occasion of a Test match, especially one involving those oldest of antagonists, England and Australia, creates its own special atmosphere. And when a young player, on his début, introduces himself to a wider audience with a spectacular performance, that atmosphere is further charged with shared excitement at such immediate success and with the expectation of being present at the launching of a brilliant career. 'I was there', they can say, 'when Botham took five wickets against Australia in his first Test match.' Four of those wickets came in a 34-ball spell which cost just 13 runs.

Ian Botham has always enjoyed his tussles with the Australians. Of his 300 Test wickets, more than a third have been against them. In 1977, he returned from a winter in Melbourne on a Whitbread Scholarship to help Somerset defeat Greg Chappell's touring side. Typically Botham, he was in action from first to last, catching McCosker off the fifth ball of the match and seeing Somerset to victory with an hour to spare with 39 of an unbroken stand of 53 with Phil Slocombe. In between he had taken five wickets and struck three sixes and six fours in his first-innings 59.

The Australians got the upper hand when Ian played for MCC against them at Lord's where his bowling was sufficiently undisciplined for England not to risk him in the one-day Prudential Trophy matches, though he was in the squad and 12th man at The Oval. His Test call-up came for the third Test at Trent Bridge later in the year, but had Chris Old not withdrawn from the team because of injury, Ian might again have found himself carrying the drinks.

He could not have chosen a more auspicious match to begin his England career. Geoffrey Boycott had been included in the side for the first time after three years of self-imposed exile, the gates were closed before lunch on the first day for the first time at Nottingham since Bradman's farewell tour of 1948, and that afternoon The Queen visited the ground as part of her Silver Jubilee celebrations. By then, thanks to radio and television, the name of Botham was on many lips. Lucky, some of them said, recalling Phil Edmonds's five-wicket début at Headingley against the 1975 Australians.

Luck, however, comes to those who seek it, and Ian was prepared from the outset to buy his wickets if necessary. The half-volley on the off-stump begged to be driven; but the late away swing might take an edge for the waiting slips. At Headingley, in his second Test, he and Mike Hendrick made short work of the Australian first innings as the ball swung in and away under a helpful cloud cover. Once more Ian claimed five wickets – for just 21 runs: in the second innings, as at Trent Bridge, he failed to take a wicket. Indeed he did not even finish the match.

Troubled for several weeks by twinges in his left foot (diagnosed after X-rays as a strained ligament), on the fourth and final day at Headingley he put out a foot to stop the ball, trod on it awkwardly and fractured the bone linking the third toe to the rest of his foot. He spent the last weeks of the season in plaster but was chosen for the side to tour Pakistan and New Zealand that winter.

Ian failed to reclaim his Test place in Pakistan, but an unbeaten 126 at Christchurch against Canterbury, with three-quarters of his runs coming in boundaries, saw him back for the first Test against New Zealand. England lost that match – their first defeat by New Zealand – but thanks to Botham's pugnacious attitude in adversity they won the next Test, in Christchurch, to square the series. It could be said that he won the match himself: the first in a series of 'Botham's Tests'.

He began with a maiden Test century, 103, resplendent with powerful strokes, which was the basis of England's recovery from 26 for three to 418. It contained one six and twelve fours. In the second innings, with England needing runs quickly for a declaration, he showed his appreciation of the situation by running out his captain, Boycott, and hitting 30 off 36 balls. With the ball he took five wickets in New Zealand's first innings and three in their second, as well as three superb catches – diving ones at slip and leg slip and finally a running catch at square leg, following a dash from leg slip, to remove the obdurate Richard Hadlee.

Already on the tour a rivalry had developed between these two young lions. It was as if both knew that over the coming years the title of 'Best all-rounder in the world' would be disputed between them. It was more than just coincidence that in 1984, when Hadlee became the first player to do 'the double' in an English season for 17 years, it was Ian Botham's Somerset who beat Hadlee's Nottinghamshire in the final match of the Championship to prevent the Trent Bridge men from taking the county title. Fate has a great affinity for cricket. In the drawn third Test, Ian again captured five wickets (for 109 runs) and enlivened a pedestrian England innings with attacking strokes in his half-century.

When New Zealand visited England later in 1978, Botham was at the height of his bowling powers, taking 24 wickets in the three-match series at 14.04 apiece: nine at Trent Bridge and 11 at Lord's. In the first series of the English summer, against a Pakistan side denuded of their key World Series Cricket players, he had run riot: two successive centuries and 13 wickets, including 108 and eight for 34 at Lord's, an unprecedented feat in a Test match. In his 11 Tests to the end of that 1978 season, he had hit three centuries and taken five wickets in an innings eight times. He was fit, at times he bowled with genuine speed, and he batted with awesome power and a cavalier approach. He looked unstoppable.

The winter tour to Australia, however, did see a tightening of the reins. Despite beginning the tour with an injury, having cut his wrist when he plunged his hand through glass in a door, he was still England's leading wicket-taker. But at 24.65 each, his 23 wickets in the six-Test series were more expensive, and while there were two half-centuries, there was no hundred in his 291 runs. Against a second, even third-strength Australian team he had not proved to hardened Australians that he was the all-conquering hero of his advance notices. On the other hand, experienced watchers should have noticed and noted the controlled aggression which Botham showed at Adelaide as his 74 transformed an ominous 18 for four into an England total of 169, and how his four wickets helped prevent Australia from gaining a first-innings lead. England, ably generalled by Mike Brearley, the wise hand resting on Botham's broad shoulders went on to win this match and clinch the series with a 205-run victory.

His first Test – England's third against Australia that summer, and Botham has a wonderful start. Five wickets in his first innings, including those of Greg Chappell (left) and Rod Marsh (above).

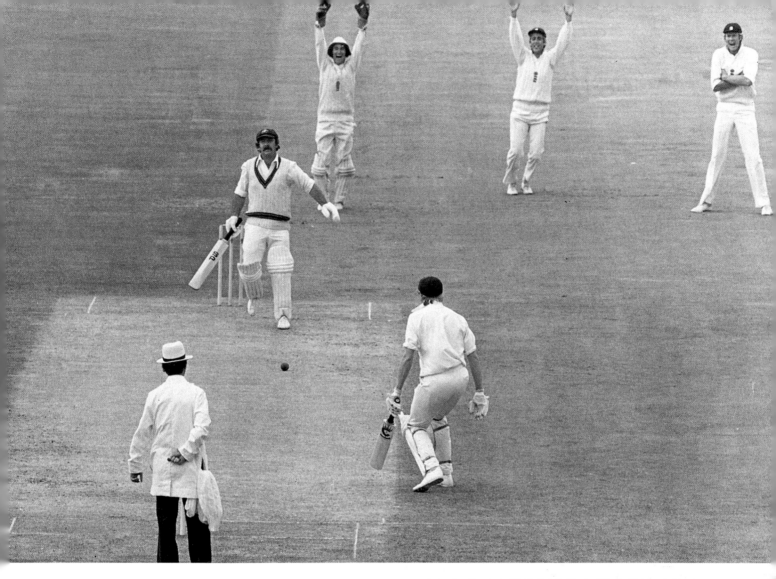

Randall, Brearley, Hendrick, Greig and Knott
congratulate the newcomer.

A big moment for the young all-rounder; ap-
plauded from the scene of his first Test
triumph by his team mates and to a standing
ovation from the Trent Bridge crowd. Among
the players is Tony Greig (left) who had been
the 'golden boy' of English cricket and captain
of his adoptive country but was shortly to leave
for the Packer circus. Before another year had
passed, such was Botham's impact, no one
concerned himself over the former hero's ineli-
gibility.

Ian made 25 in his first Test innings, sharing in partnerships with Alan Knott and Derek Underwood.

The fourth Test against Australia, Botham's second, was at Headingley. Once again the newcomer took five wickets in an innings. Umpire Bill Alley (of New South Wales and Somerset) has just given David Hookes out lbw (right).

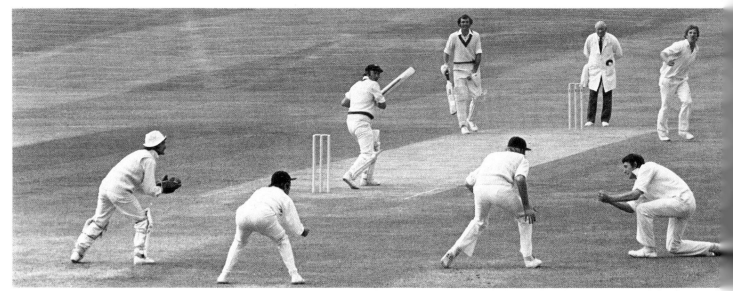

Jeff Thomson, the fifth victim, is bowled as Australia are routed in their first innings.

A classic set piece (left) as Mike Hendrick at third slip holds a chance offered by Doug Walters, always fallible in England against the moving ball.

Botham wintered with England on tour for the first time in 1977-78. He did not get a Test in Pakistan (above), but played his way into the side in New Zealand, where he made his first Test hundred to help England square the series.

On his return to England he scored his second Test century – exactly 100 – against Pakistan at Edgbaston (below and right).

He followed this with another century at Lord's. *Overleaf*: Miandad wisely gets out of the way

Not content with a century, Botham put in a remarkable spell to demolish the Pakistani second innings. Of the eight wickets, seven are pictured here. The first was Mudassar Nazar caught Taylor 10 (above).

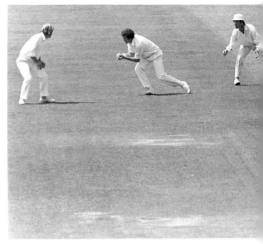

Talat Ali, caught Roope 40

Haroon Rashid, bowled 4

Wasim Raja, caught and bowled 1

Wasim Bari, caught Taylor 1

Sikander Bakht, caught Roope 1

Iqbal Qasim, bowled 0

One of many examples of Botham having failed with bat but succeeding with ball was the Trent Bridge Test against New Zealand. Having made eight, he took six wickets in the first innings (nine in the match). Geoff Howarth ended up with no more than a sore head (left and below) after ducking into a bouncer.

Above: Ian holds Howarth off Hendrick at second slip.

Mike Brearley always seemed to bring the best out of this remarkable all-rounder. When not celebrating a wicket off his own bowling, he was holding catches off others'.

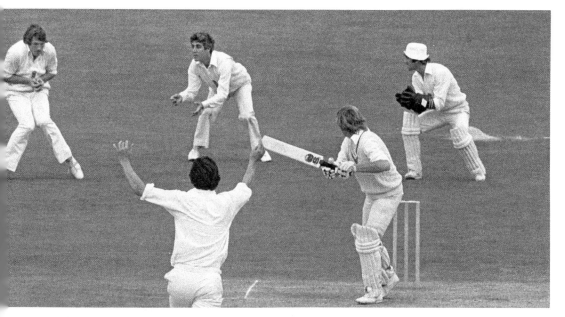

Bruce Edgar is caught at forward short leg off Phil Edmonds; a different fielding position, a different type of catch.

Typical of the enthusiasm with which Botham throws himself around the field was this run-out of Richard Hadlee at Lord's. Following through from his own bowling he raced Hadlee up the pitch until the stumps were at point-blank range, whereupon he launched himself and ball unerringly at the target.

Christmas is never the best time to be away from home. However, the England team, who have more practice than most at making the best of Christmas overseas, celebrate with a fancy dress lunch. Cameramen are allowed a glimpse. In this case Chris Old's furry friend (left) is none other than Guy the Gorilla (right).

Next day, it's business as usual, for the Melbourne Test traditionally starts on Boxing Day. Kim Hughes has been caught by Gower, and the bowler plays to the crowd.

3

Test-Match Double

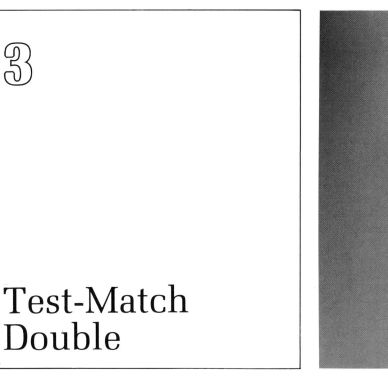

When, on a sunny Birmingham Friday, Ian Botham walked out to take guard for the first time in the 1979 series against India, a glance at his Test record revealed 791 Runs and 87 wickets. Given a success rate in the four Tests equal to his achievements in three against Pakistan the previous year, he would at 23 complete 1,000 runs and take his 100th wicket for England: the fastest in time and Tests, as well as the youngest, to perform this Test-match double.

His target was the 23 Tests in six years of the Indian all-rounder Vinoo Mankad: the fastest English double was Maurice Tate's in 33 Tests, the same number taken by that great Australian competitor, Keith Miller. Gary Sobers had to wait until his 48th Test. Botham's double, when he achieved it at The Oval in his 21st Test, came in his third year as an England player. Even taking into account the fecundity of Tests in the modern age, it was a phenomenal performance: the realisation of boundless enthusiasm, a natural ability bordering on genius, and an unquenchable self-belief.

In 1977, the year of his England début, Ian had had another double in his sights: 1,000 runs and 100 wickets in an English season. Test selection handicapped and injury prevented that: when his leg went into plaster he had

scored 738 runs and taken 88 wickets. As he sought his first Test double before the Indians left England, his greatest problem, midway through the series, looked like being his obtaining the runs he required. Batting at No. 6, with the likes of Boycott, Gooch, Gower and Randall ahead of him, he had had few opportunities for the big hundred that would launch his attempt. At Edgbaston, where Boycott (155) and Gower (200 not out) dominated England's only innings, Ian scored 33; at Lord's, 36.

On the Monday of Lord's, however, he did claim his 100th Test wicket in the shortest time on record – though not in the fewest Tests. George Lohman, the Surrey medium-pacer of the 19th century, took his 100th wicket in his 16th Test, while 'Charlie' Blythe, Kent's slow left-armer who died in action in the First World War, also captured 100 wickets in 19 Tests, the same as Botham. In the first innings, Ian had taken five wickets for the 10th time in his Test career, his five for 35 following his five for 70 in India's second innings at Birmingham.

The 100th wicket was a prized one: that of Sunil Gavaskar, the little Indian master. Already in the same over he had been allowed a life: though perhaps only Randall at cover could have turned that mistimed square cut into a chance. The next delivery, a good sharp Botham bouncer lifting into Gavaskar's chest, was played just short of

Brearley at first slip; the fourth ball beat him outside the off stump as he felt for it.

In one over, the emphasis had changed. Where previously Gavaskar's impetuous strokeplay had brought him a heady fifty, suddenly the ball held sway. Unsettled, over-ambitious, Gavaskar now drove at a ball too low of bounce and it nicked the bottom edge of the bat: as the eye adjusted Brearley was falling back, the ball taken low in his left hand. Botham, the bull who had beaten the matador, thrust his fists like horns to the heavens in triumph.

Two Tests later, in India's first innings at The Oval, Ian himself took a more spectacular catch, reacting with speed of mind and body when Bairstow, the wicketkeeper, parried a chance from Vengsarkar on to Brearley's boot, whence it ricocheted up to be snatched one-handed by Botham moving from second slip. His 10 catches in the series were the most by a player on either side. Indeed, it seemed impossible to keep the man out of the limelight. Off the second ball he faced at The Oval, cut backward of point for four off Bedi, he had scored the three runs needed for his 1,000 runs. And on the final day, with India moving towards a fourth-innings victory target of 438, he transformed the state of the game with a catch, a run-out and three wickets in the last 12 overs so that, with three balls remaining, any one of four results was possible: victory to either side, tie or draw. Ultimately it was the draw. True, he did drop Vengsarkar on the boundary when India were 365 for one – but annoyance at his fallibility motivated him. Brearley, knowing his man, brought him back on to bowl with eight overs remaining and Botham took three wickets for 17, including the crucial one of Gavaskar when he had scored 221.

This series, after the World Cup in which Ian did little of note, confirmed his status as a Test-match all-rounder but also gave rise to a feeling that the one-day game was not really his métier; certainly not at international level. He needed the time and the scope of a Test match to stamp his mark on the proceedings; the fluctuations of fortune. He relished the breadth of the larger canvas.

Botham, or such was the impression he gave, would rather bowl a different ball with every delivery in the hope of a wicket. Not for him containment with every six, unless perchance they were bowled to Viv Richards: then containment could be a challenge. Mike Hendrick, with whom Ian enjoyed a friendship enveloping a shared love of the English countryside as well as the fellowship of cricket, was the ideal one-day bowler, never deviating from a remorseless line and length. But tellingly he never once took five wickets in an innings in his 30 Test matches.

Batting at No. 6 for England in one-day games, when the call is for accelerating the run-rate, Ian rarely had the chance to play as he did in Tests. For essentially he is not, never has been, a slogger. In the nets he might set his sights on the pavilion windows or a passing housing estate, but in the middle the ball is played on its merit – or Ian's assessment of its merit. His powerful hitting emanates from the timing of his strokes as much as from the strength of his limbs and torso. He is not, despite the expectations of the incognoscente, the village blacksmith.

The marvellous hitting of his Headingley century against the Indians, for example, which took him to within three runs of his Test-match double, was violent and yet at the same time calculated. There were five sixes, massive blows, one sweep off the left-arm spin of Bedi carrying into the car park. There were 16 fours. Yet when defence was called for, Ian was as unpassable as a Bailey.

His innings occupied two and three-quarter hours of a match which, paralysed by bad weather and the timidity of officialdom from half an hour after lunch on the first day (when Ian was nine not out) until the fourth morning, lasted only 11 hours and 40 minutes. It – Ian Botham – breathed life into a game seemingly dead as no man in England could. When he was out, courageously caught at cover by Ghavri, it seemed appropriate that he should go attempting the boundary which would have brought his 1,000 runs, rather than seeking them in safe singles. It was a Botham end to one of the great Botham innings.

Net practice at Lord's. Anyone who has watched Botham in the nets will be aware of his attitude to being caged. On this occasion the target was an innocent clock some 90 yards away.

Every ball is a potential victim. The crowd enjoy the moment as much as the batsman. Most bowlers suffer as the ball generally has to be recovered from a great distance.

This one (*above*) is an attempt on a groundsman's window – a temporary change of target. The ultimate accolade (*right*) – a grin for the one that just couldn't be hit.

The first major landmark in sight. Botham's 99th Test victim was Reddy, lbw in India's first innings at Lord's. The next wicket, for this photographer at least, was a long time coming.

After only 19 Tests Ian becomes the youngest ever cricketer to take 100 Test wickets. His victim, impressively enough, was Sunil Gavaskar caught by Mike Brearley at first slip.

Now chasing his thousandth run in Test cricket, Botham nearly succeeded in the Leeds Test following that at Lord's. He made 137, an innings remembered most for the massive sixes he hit off Bedi. Here he does not neglect the possibilities of the swiftly run ones and twos when facing Kapil Dev.

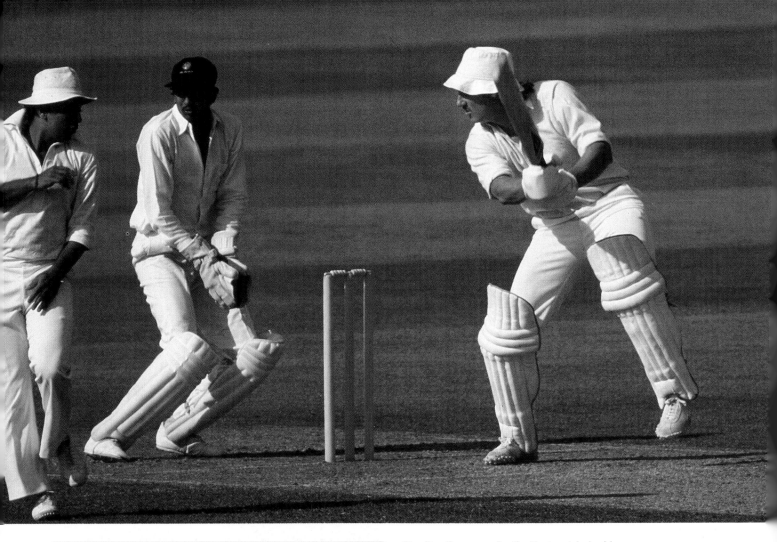

Needing three runs for the Test match double, Ian square cuts Bishen Bedi for four. Congratulations are in order from partner Graham Gooch (right) and the great Indian spinner himself (left). Botham took only 21 Tests to complete 1000 runs and 100 wickets.

While his England exploits captured the head-lines, Botham continued to excite and frustrate his Somerset supporters. In 1979 Somerset won the Gillette Cup, playing both the semi-final and final at Lord's.

In the semi-final (right) he beat the bat often enough in a brilliant opening spell, but ended up without a single wicket.

In the final against Northamptonshire he made 27 (below), was again wicketless, but was as enthusiastic as any of his colleagues in congra-tulating Garner on the dismissal of Larkins (right).

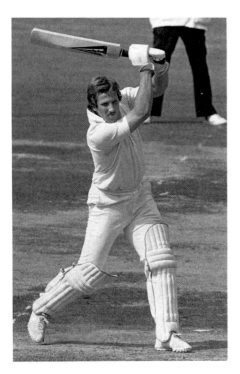

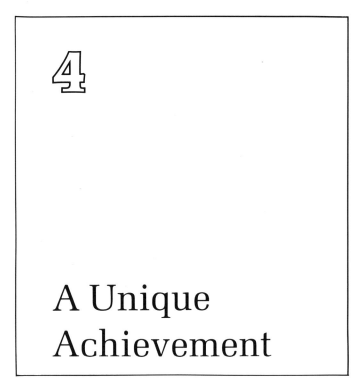

4

A Unique Achievement

England's second successive summer in Australia followed the resumption of peace in the cricket world earlier in 1979. The Australian Cricket Board, estimated to have lost some £445,000 during the two-year dispute with Kerry Packer's World Series Cricket camp, had about-turned and come to terms with their former adversary; indeed, had agreed that PBL Sports, a Packer off-shoot, would have the right to promote 'the programme of cricket organised by the Board' and arrange its televising and merchandising.

The 1979-80 season was their first venture. And if there was still any question as to which was the dog and which was the tail in Australian cricket, it was quickly answered when India, whom the Board had invited to tour Australia in 1979-80, along with England, were asked to defer their visit so that West Indies, brim-full with exciting performers, could top the bill in PBL's inaugural season.

The subsequent twin tours were, to be honest, a hotch-potch of cricket: worst of all for Australia, who played two three-Test series against England and West Indies concurrently as well as contesting the also concurrently running Benson and Hedges World Series Cup one-day competition. They were virtually a touring team in their own country. However, they did know the conditions. The

England players, although most of them had been in Australia a year before, still had to acclimatise: and such a tour, with its emphasis on Test matches and one-day internationals, provided few opportunities. Even England's beginning-of-tour practice was curtailed to one full session because of heavy rain in Sydney.

Ian Botham, while becoming less and less inclined to use the nets as a means of sorting out his game, none the less needed practice and warm-up games as much as the others. His bowling, for example, required a different approach from in England, where the conditions encouraged seam and swing bowling of a full length. The harder Australian wickets under cloudless skies required something less full of length, while his out-swinger's line had to be adjusted from the stumps to just outside off stump if it was to take the edge of the driving bat. Only at Sydney, where the decision to give the ground staff a day off to celebrate New Year resulted in the pitch being exposed to a thunderstorm, was Ian able to bowl an English line and length; and his figures in Australia's first innings in the second Test – 17-7-29-4 – recount his control and success there. In England's first innings he was top-scorer with 27 after Greg Chappell had put them in on the damp and patchy pitch.

Botham's best bowling in Australia, though, had come

already: in the first Test at Perth. With Hendrick out of the tour with a shoulder injury after only four overs of the opening game, and with Willis operating as 'third seamer' rather than firing the attack, Ian had to fill the role of both strike and stock bowler: 35 overs in Australia's first innings with six wickets for 78; 45.5 overs in their second with five for 98. Five wickets in a Test innings for the 11th and 12th time; 10 in a match for the second time – and his first against Australia. It was a superlative demonstration of Botham's physical and mental determination on an occasion when his team and his captain Brearley called for his all. He gave it willingly and courageously.

His reward, after a one-day international against West Indies in Brisbane and Christmas plus a day-nighter against Australia in Sydney, was his first taste of captaincy since his schooldays. To his unashamed enjoyment, his England XI beat Queensland – back in Brisbane – by 138 runs. His own contribution, however, was slight: 21 and five; under instructions from the tour management he did not bowl. But it was his batting that was giving rise to concern, especially for assistant-manager Ken Barrington.

Apart from 76 in 94 minutes in a non first-class match against Combined Universities early in the tour, that 27 in the second Test at Sydney was his highest score until then in any form of the game. When he followed it with a second-innings duck, it was obvious that his technique, as well as his attitude, was at fault. Neither could be solved easily, because all that fell between the second and third Tests were four one-day internationals, followed by a three-day match against New South Wales. (In the event, Ian was rested for the state game.)

Ian's approach to his batting had much to do with the nature of the tour. Basically he was trying to thump everything in sight as if he was batting in the final overs of a one-day match: which for much of the tour he had been.

It was only in the last match of the World Series Cup, when he hit 37 off 39 balls against West Indies, that the Botham bat had a resounding ring to it. And by then Ian and Barrington had sorted out the technical problems. Earlier Ian had been going too far across his stumps: all right for the drives he favoured but leaving him off balance and off line when playing balls pitched on middle and leg. On Barrington's advice he changed his guard from middle and leg to leg stump; and in the Melbourne Test, in his last innings in Australia, he was able to provide evidence down under of his true all-round worth.

When he came in to bat in the second innings, the position was not promising for a major innings. England, 171 behind on first innings, were 88 for five and soon to be 92 for six when Brearley went. Only the tail remained; but remain they did. Ian, going mostly on to the front foot to counter the low bounce and driving forcefully whenever possible, saw England to 157 at stumps. Next day he fulfilled all the hopes of his admirers, scoring 70 of the 93 runs in the morning session. Taylor (32) added but a few to his overnight score; Underwood, Lever (12 in 106 minutes) and Willis contributed just 14 as Ian put on 95 with them for the last three wickets. His unbeaten 119, his fifth Test hundred, saved England from an innings defeat, though he was unable to prevent Australia from making a clean sweep of the series.

On then to Bombay for the Test to celebrate the Golden Jubilee of the Indian Board of Control: but first the nightmarish moments of two aborted take-offs at Perth. An overcast sky and a grassy wicket must have made the Wankhede Stadium look like Headingley after Australia, and Botham revelled in the conditions, turning the match into a celebration of his own marvellous talents.

Six wickets as India were dismissed on the first day; a century (114) to ensure England's recovery on the second and third days; another seven wickets as India were bowled out a second time on the third and fourth. John Arlott's introductory essay contains the figures; Patrick Eagar's photos have captured the action. No similar all-round performance had been recorded; and until Imran Khan scored 117 and took 11 wickets for Pakistan against India three years later, Ian Botham was unique in the history of Test cricket.

On tour again, England visited Australia in the winter of 1979-80. It was the first 'post-Packer' tour; three sides, England, Australia and West Indies, competing in one-day internationals against each other and the two visiting teams playing Test matches against Australia.

In the Sydney Test Ian had a poor time with the bat (left) but took four first-innings wickets, and caught the former Australian captain Ian Chappell for Derek Underwood's 100th Australian victim in Tests.

England upset the promoters by qualifying for the Grand Final of the one-day series. (The script had Australia in their place for the three match decider.) Under the lights at Sydney England lost to West Indies for a second time, thus obviating the need for the third match.

Fielding in twilight has its problems. In pain after being struck on the knee, Botham waits for medical aid (left).

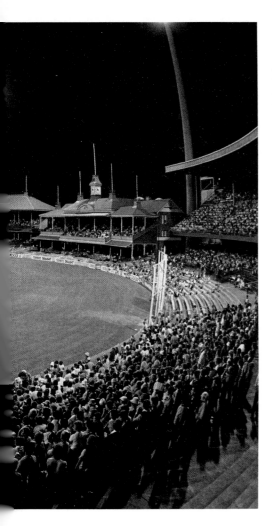

Dark blue pads are the order of the day, or night, as Ian thumps the white ball around for 37 runs. It wasn't enough as England lost to the world champions by eight wickets.

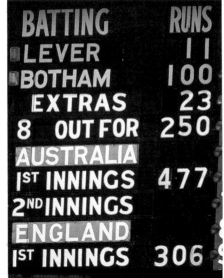

There was little to cheer about for an England supporter on this visit to Australia. The highlight was Botham's century in the third Test against Australia at Melbourne. He took three wickets in the first innings and followed this with his first hundred against Australia.

On their way home from Australia, England called in at Bombay to play a Jubilee Test against India. For Botham it turned out to be an all-round 'tour de force'.

Sandip Patil is caught Taylor (left) and Ian attempts a soccer-style run-out (below) as he takes six first-innings wickets.

By one of those freaks of Test match programming, the Australian cricket team, en route for Pakistan, were able to watch a day's play while on a stop-over in Bombay. Botham and Lillee exchange anecdotes (right).

Cricket in Bombay is hot work, certainly so if you have bowled virtually unchanged in the second innings to add a match total of 13 wickets to a first-innings century – something never before done in the history of Test cricket. Also in the photograph, on the right, is Bob Taylor who, in taking 10 catches, also created a world record.

Opposite: Ian batting during his 114 at Bombay. In this innings which turned England's 58 for five into a match-winning 229 for six, Botham completed five wickets and a century in a match for a record third time.

Left: Not content with his performance so far, Ian bowled unchanged in India's second innings, apart from one over when he changed ends, and took seven wickets.

Below: Bob Taylor holds Sunil Gavaskar for his ninth catch of the match.

5

Captain
of England

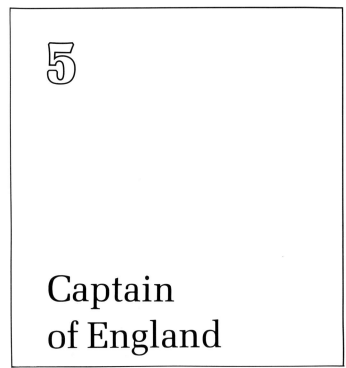

'Cricket's man of the decade but captain of nobody' wrote one national newspaper when Ian Botham was named, in mid-May of 1980, as England's captain for the two Prudential Trophy matches against West Indies. But, while adding that Ian was on trial, England's chairman of selectors, Alec Bedser, seemed unpeturbed by his lack of experience. 'Botham brings a brand of brilliance and ebullience to the job', he said. And when Ian hit the winning runs at Lord's and England won by three wickets to square the one-day series, the selectors' faith seemed justified. None the less they maintained caution, making him captain for only the first two Tests. At 24, he was to be England's youngest Test captain since the 23-year-old Ivo Bligh led England against Australia in 1882-83.

Botham's elevation to the Captaincy followed upon the reluctance of Mike Brearley to tour again. Brearley could have remained captain for the 1980 series, but the selectors had also to consider the coming winter's tour to West Indies. A summer's experience for a new captain was better than no experience at all.

Did it have to be Botham? Obviously he was the outstanding player. Of the other names mentioned, Keith Fletcher was suspect against the fastest bowling; Roger Knight, the Surrey captain, was not of Test standard – and the strongest team was needed; and Geoffrey Boycott's previous captaincy of England did not really encourage a second tenure.

Botham's own county captain, Brian Rose, since last playing for England in 1978, had in 1979 led Somerset to their first major county titles – the Gillette Cup and John Player league – and enjoyed a successful season with the bat. However, his rating in the selectors' reckoning became apparent early in the season when their chairman, in Rose's presence, was critical of those counties who appointed captains who could not go on to captain England. Somerset had made Rose their captain in 1978. Such is the irony of life, and of cricket, that when Rose was called up for the third Test, at Old Trafford, he matched the West Indian fast bowling with splendid aggression for a top score of 70; indeed, went on to top the England averages for the series.

Just as irony is an ingredient in life's pudding, so too is luck: and while Dame Fortune had ridden easily on Ian Botham's shoulders for some seasons, now without warning she deserted him. In England's first innings of the first Test, when he top-scored with 57, she was there when he was dropped in the slip cordon at 20; and when Joel Garner, his Somerset team-mate, split his helmet. For this indignity, Garner and Roberts were both hit into the crowd. When England restricted West Indies' lead to 45, the new captain had good reason for satisfaction.

But a second innings of 252, after England had been 174 for two, was disappointing. Worse still for Botham, England's slow batting had allowed Viv Richards, deputising as captain for the injured Clive Lloyd, to gain ascendancy in the captaincy stakes. Nevertheless, with the ball moving about, West Indies' target of 208 in four sessions was not going to come easily if England's captain could maintain the pressure.

Richards took the initiative with a blistering 48 in 56 minutes, but Ian trapped him in front with a leg-cutter just before the close so that West Indies began the final day requiring 99 runs with eight wickets in hand. Immediately it was seven wickets as Bacchus went first ball. Willis, with great heart, bowled on and on, chipping away at the innings. Roberts, coming in at 180 for seven, chanced his arm and had reduced the margin to 13 when, slogging at Willis, he was dropped by Gower, usually the safest of hands, at cover. Imperceptibly England heads went down. They still fought, but one had the feeling . . . . If only then. Victory instead of the eventual defeat, would have set an extra spring in Botham's stride, making him sure in his own mind that he was the man for the job.

Although Ian's captaincy was confirmed after the drawn second Test (the remaining Tests were drawn) and he took England to the West Indies, his unexpected loss of form became a cause for concern. His style was to lead from the front, but the big innings or the five-wicket returns which would have inspired his team never came.

It did not help that throughout 1980 he was never fully fit. Coming in to bowl, troubled by a back injury, he looked laboured. His 40 first-class wickets that season, at 34.67 apiece, represented his leanest return since 1974 – his first season. And though his batting had begun with a blaze of runs – 647 for Somerset before the first Test at the beginning of June – from 4 June to 3 August he did not have a single Championship innings for them. Small wonder that he complained of being unable to bat himself into form for the Test matches.

In the West Indies, the story was much the same; though England's leading wicket-taker (15), he was more expensive than of yore (32.80); he was bowling without rhythm, yet dismissive when asked about his fitness. (Before the tour he had had to pass a fitness test.) His batting was a great disappointment; a mere 73 runs in the four Tests; wanting in technique and concentration. His catching, in the past so brilliant, was now unsure. By the end of the tour it seemed that his confidence had gone.

Off the field, on the other hand, his easy manner ensured good relations between his side and their hosts; and despite the problems of bad weather early in the tour which kept players idle, the uncertainty about the tour when Guyana refused to accept Robin Jackman because of his South African connections, and the tragic death of the much-loved Ken Barrington, Botham led a happy touring party. Any captain would have found it a taxing tour; let alone one still new to the job and for the first time abandoned by his own enormous talents.

In the circumstances England's two-nil defeat, against a superior side, was not a disaster. Less palatable was their tepid showing in the first two Tests of 1981 against Kim Hughes's Australians. Starting as underdogs, despite their taking the one-day series two-one, Australia won the first Test at Trent Bridge by four wickets in four days. England's catching, such a feature of the Brearley era, was abject: at least six chances went to ground in Australia's first innings alone.

The Lord's Test, the second, was drawn, but just as disappointing as Botham's two ducks, the first pair of his Test career, was the fact that at times England looked rudderless. There coule be no escaping the feeling that a new captain was needed. The selectors had begun the series by reappointing Ian on a Test-by-Test basis: understandable in the circumstances but unsatisfactory for the player and his team. For his own peace of mind, and because he could see how the adverse press comments and the uncertainty of his situation were affecting his family, Ian sought the confidence of the selectors: the captaincy for the remaining four Tests. When it was not forthcoming he resigned; it was the end of a fruitless year.

The scene is Lord's and it is net practice on the day before Ian's first appearance there as England captain. Geoffrey Boycott – opening bat, elder statesman and former captain – was available for advice and discussion.

Botham charges for the pavilion, having won his first Lord's international match as captain. The two-match Prudential Trophy series was won by West Indies on faster run rate.

Ian Botham starts off on the right foot in his first Test as England captain by winning the toss against Clive Lloyd.

Excitement mounted on the last day as Bob Willis took five wickets and set England on course for an improbable victory. Here he bowls Malcolm Marshall. However Andy Roberts, batting with Desmond Haynes, saw West Indies home with two wickets to spare.

West Indies have been near impossible to beat for some time. Ian's task as captain was to minimise the damage and to enjoy any moments of success that might follow.

At Old Trafford he has Kallicharran caught by Knott (above) and uproots Viv Richards' leg stump (left). Earlier he had brilliantly caught Bacchus at second slip off Dilley (below).

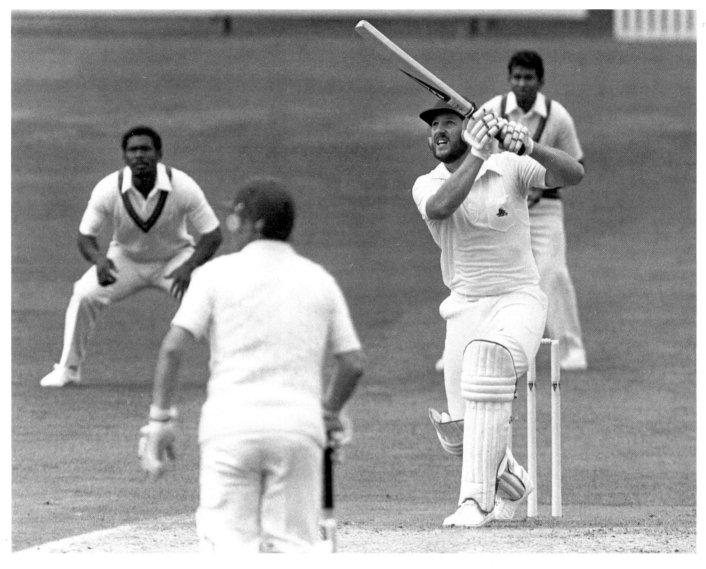

Botham mis-hits a drive off Holding to Viv Richards, at mid-off, who enjoys catching his Somerset team-mate in the fifth Test of the series at Headingley (this page).

Opposite – "If it's so damn easy, why don't you have a go?" Cricket, hardly ever a simple game on the field especially when you are captaining your country again West Indies, looks rather easier when viewed from the bar.

In the ceremonial before play on the Saturday of the Centenary Test, Ian takes his place at the end of a long and distinguished line of English and Australian captains (above).

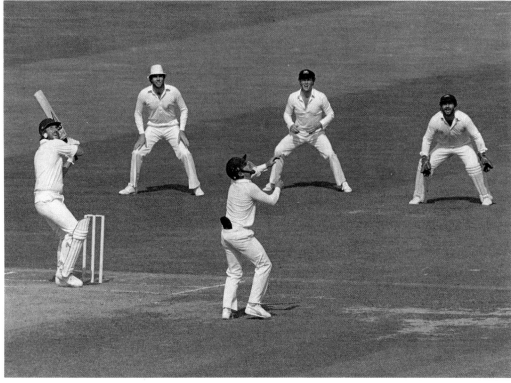

Following a full series against Clive Lloyd's West Indians, the Centenary Test against Australia at Lord's must have seemed light relief. Perhaps too light as Botham skies Pascoe to be caught by Wood (left).

Less than four months after the last Test against West Indies, the team move off to the Caribbean for another five Tests against Clive Lloyd's side. Here, at the farewell meeting at Lord's, Ian and Ken Barrington, who was not to return home, joke with Roland Butcher.

England ran into a full-scale political row when, following the injured Willis' return home, they sent for Robin Jackman as a replacement bowler. Jackman was unacceptable to the Guyanese authorities and was deported. The England team all left together and are seen above at Georgetown airport.

Such moments are difficult for all, and an unusually contemplative Ian Botham (left) shows the cares of captaincy while waiting in the lobby of the Pegasus Hotel.

For some days there was doubt as to whether the tour would continue. Ian, along with the rest of the team, whiled away the time at their Barbados beach hotel (right).

Who else could Botham have caught in the first innings of the Barbados Test but Viv Richards? This special war dance is reserved for none other. Gooch (centre) and Emburey (right) join in.

England's turn to bat and the bouncers and helmets fly. Holding, Roberts, Garner and Croft are no joke on the Kensington Oval pitch.

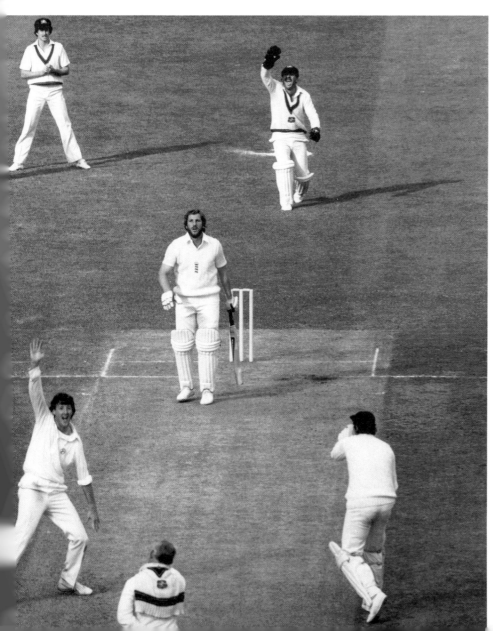

After 10 Tests against West Indies, with only the Centenary Test at Lord's against Australia in between, the strain was beginning to tell. It was probably "mission impossible" but by his own high standards Ian was disappointed with his side's performance and must now have begun to doubt his luck, if not his ability.

In the first two Tests of the Ashes summer Ian was bowled Alderman for 1 at Trent Bridge (top left); made 33 in the second innings; at Lord's was lbw to Lawson for 0 (left) and in the second innings was bowled by Bright for a first-ball duck (above). At an all-time low in terms of personal performance, and following much press criticism, he resigned from the captaincy of England.

6

National Hero

There are occasions in life which suspend action, thoughts and emotions long enough for time never to dispel them. They may be on a world scale, such as the declaration of a war or an assassination; they may be personal. What they all have in common, regardless, is the perspicuity of recall; not only of the occasion itself but also, quite vividly, of one's own whereabouts and actions at the time. Such was the impact of the happening. So it was for many in that marvellous season of Ian Botham's when he, single-handed it seemed, won the Ashes series against Australia in 1981.

His deeds, of course, are already part of cricket's history and its legend: the latter will grow with the decades while the former is documented in detail on paper and film. And for those who were in England at the time, not just lovers of cricket but men and women from all walks of life; for these, what Ian Botham did is etched in the memory. Brearley, sharp of intellect and subtle with men, may have been the Messiah, and Willis, with his fixed eyes and his creaking knees, may have been the essential of the Headingley victory; but while the sun shone through the months of July and August, the name on the lips of the common man was Botham.

Yet few would have been there to see him play those wonderful innings of Headingley and Old Trafford; their thoughts would have been somewhere between Sunday lunch and Sunday tea when, with five for one in 28 deliveries, he bowled Australia to defeat at Edgbaston. A great number would have watched them on television and rejoiced as Botham himself rejoiced in the unleashing of his talents with a grin, a laugh of wolvish proportion. Others would only have read of them as their newspapers proclaimed again and again his name, and the talk of clerks at their desks and boys at their barrows would have been of Botham as once it would have been of Nelson.

The headiest achievements I did not see: other than on television. I had been at the first Test, which Australia won, and at Lord's where all was discontent and Botham, sadly but not unexpectedly, stood down as captain. Then other work kept me away from cricket until the fifth match of the series, at Old Trafford.

None the less those three days, two at Headingley and the Sunday at Edgbaston, stand as clear in the memory as when, half asleep, I heard someone say in an adjoining room, 'Kennedy's been shot'.

On the Monday afternoon of Headingley I was reading proofs of a football book: a tiresome job requiring full concentration and endless cups of coffee. Every so many galleys I would check the state of play on the radio: it was really just a question of when England would lose and by how much. So when Botham came in to join Boycott, at his defensive best, what made me go through to another room to turn on the television? A desire to witness the last rites; boredom with the task in hand; some writer's instinct? An over or two passed: nothing happened to convince me that Boycott or Botham would do anything other than delay the inevitable. I returned to my proofs, leaving the television on so that, glancing up, I might see what was happening.

Boycott looked displeased as he was walking off, whether with himself or the lbw decision I couldn't say – and the commentators had been muted. Taylor must have gone quickly: next time I looked up Botham was leaning on his bat, contemplating the incoming Dilley. They had a bit of a chat and a laugh; the Australians settled for the kill; I took up my coffee and turned to watch.

Graham Dilley I'd always liked as a cricketer. He looked as if he enjoyed the game. At Trent Bridge, in the first Test, his 34 was England's second-highest score: a sensibly but briskly played knock. Tall and left-handed, he drove through the covers like some modern Woolley when bat and leg chose to follow the same line – which wasn't always. And he could thump the ball. Botham, in long-sleeved sweater and hatless in contrast to Dilley's short sleeves and blue helmet, enjoyed every moment of his partner's swashbuckling while, in the field, the Australians became more ragged.

Botham's own hitting was ferocious. He hooked the labouring Lawson with relish; he cover drove, pulled and occasionally slashed; with his hair windblown, his teeth bared in a great grin and his flashing blade, he was indeed a pirate snatching from Australia's merchantmen a prize they thought was theirs.

Dilley went for 56, having put on 117 in 80 minutes with Botham: 252 for eight; Australia had to bat again but England were only 25 ahead. Old, to some surprise because he was fallible against pace, stayed while another 67 were added and Botham reached his hundred, and England ended the day 124 ahead; Botham 145 not out. Next morning he scored another four before Willis, with whom he put on 37 for the last wicket, was caught for two. By mid-afternoon Willis had taken eight for 43, career-best figures, and England were back in the series.

They went ahead in the next Test at Edgbaston. That weekend I was bricklaying: of sorts. I ran out of mortar just as Emburey bowled the ball that jumped, turned and captured Border in Australia's second innings. Consequently, on television, I saw Botham sweep aside Australia's tail, as destructive a piece of fast bowling as one would want to see. His approach to the wicket wqs eager, the bounce into the delivery stride aggressive, the delivery and follow-through clean and fast and full. The batsmen were beaten by pace: three clean-bowled, one leg-before, one caught behind. This was Botham the bowler who had seemed but a memory, responding to the cheering crowd with his own bravura.

The Old Trafford hundred (118 in 123 minutes off 102 balls) must be *the* innings of Botham's career. Twice he might have been caught: when 32 by Whitney, a high swirling chance inside the mid-off boundary, one of Botham's few mis-hits; and when 91 by Dyson, who valiantly and desperately tried to grasp a slashed square-cut as he ran from third man. Otherwise his strokeplay was powerful and pure. The bat rung and the crowd roared.

Yet it began so slowly that those late back to their seats and their cameras after lunch could miss 53 balls and 28 runs of his innings and still be in time to see the fireworks. The next 33 balls brought the carnival and the century – with a six off Bright's left-arm spin. Six sixes in all, 13 fours: it was marvellous, exhilarating, unforgettable. People walked from the ground that evening with faces red from sun and ale and wreathed in smiles. But then that was the kind of summer it had become, especially in memory. A summer of sun after a cold, grey start; a summer of smiling; and most of all of Botham laughing.

Botham was at the crease as the bookmakers quoted odds of 500-1 against England at tea on the fourth day of the Headingley Test. Seldom was a Test match more over, seldom can defeat have seemed more inevitable; seldom have so many booked out of their hotels, only to have to return. Some even decided to go home.

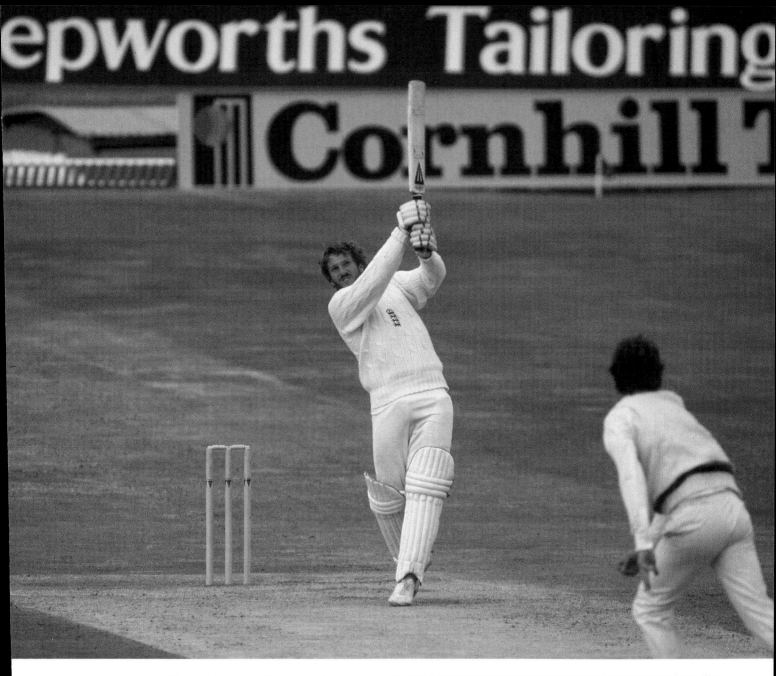

Botham's stands, first with Dilley and then with Old, are now legendary. He drove, he cut, he pulled and hooked, often with such force that it mattered not that the ball was less than perfectly struck. At times he edged the ball so outrageously that conventional field placing was out of the question.

Excerpts from this classic include a late cut off Bright (top left), his century (bottom left), a straight six off Alderman (above) and the over-night scoreboard (right).

Cornhill Insurance

ENGLAND	351-9 WKTS
BOTHAM	▥145 LWK 319
WILLIS	1 LMN 29
	B10
INNS.LD 227	OVERS85

98

145 runs later Ian weaves his way back to the England dressing-room (above).

Undefeated, he pauses for a moments private thought (left) before closing the dressing-room door on the outside world.

Botham batting in the Benson and Hedges Cup final at Lord's a week later (right). His 37 not out helped Somerset to victory over Surrey.

It's that man again. Glimpses from the next Test at Edgbaston include Ian having been caught by Marsh off Lillee for 3 (top left); taking a crucial catch – Yallop off Emburey (above); celebrating the fall of Bright (left).

Ian's final spell of five wickets in 28 balls had as superhuman a quality about it as had his innings at Leeds two weeks beforehand. Last to go was Alderman, bowled (below). England, once one down, are now one up in the series. Botham would believe the return of Brearley and of his luck were merely coincidental. Willis (right) pours the champagne.

The last of Ian's trio of unforgettable Tests was that at Old Trafford. His catch at third slip to dismiss Yallop (above) was spectacular, but it was his second innings 118 that many feel to be his greatest innings; perhaps one of the finest hundreds of the modern era.

One of its features was the hooking of Lillee with the new ball, apparently off his eyebrows (above right). More classically his square cutting (left) was accurate and decisive. When eventually he returned to the pavilion, all those present knew they had witnessed something very very special.

The series decided, the Oval Test was bound to be an anti-climax and not even Botham in his summer 1981 mood could match his own brilliance. He did manage his 200th Test wicket (right and below); Rodney Marsh caught by Mike Gatting on the boundary.

Left: Another catch at third slip, this time a rebound off Chris Tavaré to dismiss Marsh in the first innings.

Another milestone was reached on the 1981–82 tour of India: his 2000th Test run (above and right) scored in the first Test at Bombay. He was now in the elite company of Richie Benaud and Sir Gary Sobers as being the only three men in cricket history to take 200 wickets and score 2000 runs.

Ian poses for cameras at Bristol while taking a flying lesson. At an altitude of several thousand feet he does have some chance of evading the press and the publicity which all his activities tend to attract.

7

The Tide Turns

After the match-winning performances of 1981, it was hard to conceive how Ian Botham would again capture the public imagination so completely. That he never did in the year that followed was no fault of his; rather the fickleness of a general public blinded by its own concept of what Botham was as a cricketer. To the cricketing public, there was no diminution of his status as a player: only a strengthening of his claim to be the greatest all-rounder in Test-match history, although his bowling, affected more by injuries and general fitness problems, scarcely matched his often sensational batting. In just under a year, from the first Test against India in Bombay to the first Test against Australia in Perth, he was to advance his Test aggregate from 2,000 runs to 3,000 runs.

On that 1981-82 tour of India and Sri Lanka, only Graham Gooch and Chris Tavaré scored more than Botham's 760 runs at 54.28. And only Gooch (487) scored more in the six-Test series, for which Ian topped the averages with 440 runs at 55.00. There was in his batting a healthy blend of discipline and devastating aggression; and if his bowling was inconsistent and expensive, he did take most wickets in the Tests – and bowled the most overs. At Bombay, his match figures of nine for 133 off 50 overs were a deserved reward for his perseverance and immense stamina.

He began the tour, against an Indian Under-22 side, with five sixes and 10 fours in 98 off 67 balls. In the New Delhi Test, with England looking for a declaration, he hammered 66 off 48 balls, hitting five sixes; but in contrast his 142 in the Kanpur Test occupied five and a half hours and came off 214 balls. A competitive maturity was noticed.

When India toured England the following summer, 1982, he remained the bane of their bowlers. Easily England's most successful batsman, he scored almost twice as many runs as any of his team-mates, thanks to his 208 at The Oval. He was in form from the first match of the series, at Lord's where, batting at No. 5 and bristling with powerful strokes, he hit 67 and followed it with five wickets in an innings (for 46) for the 19th time in his Test career. At Old Trafford he was even better, hitting 128 off 169 balls, despite a painful blow on his left toe from a full toss by Nayak when 67. His first fifty had come off 46 balls the previous evening; after his injury he raced to his 10th Test hundred off 20 balls, seven boundaries making his runner somewhat superfluous. In all he hit two sixes and 19 fours: 'he drove, cut and pulled with brutal power', *Wisden* recorded.

For the Indians, worse followed at The Oval, where Ian

batted with a ferocious majesty. His 200 came off 220 balls in 268 minutes; his 208 contained four sixes and 19 fours. One six, a straight drive off Doshi, holed the pavilion roof. A forcing stroke off the back foot struck Gavaskar, fielding periously close at silly point, and broke his shin-bone.

In this series there was for Botham the challenge of the Indian all-rounder, Kapil Dev, and he rose to it: 403 runs at 134.33 and nine wickets at 35.55 to Kapil's 292 runs at 73.00 and 10 wickets at 43.90. But he was not as successful in the sequential series against Pakistan, captained by their own famous all-rounder, Imran Khan: Botham 163 runs at 27.16 and 18 wickets at 18.57. His best batting came at Headingley, where he made 57 out of a partnership of 69 in an hour with Gower.

Nor was that the only time in the series when Gower was dominated by Botham. At Lord's having been given the captaincy when Willis was injured, Gower often looked at a loss as Botham, over upon over, walked back to his bowling mark. If he was reluctant to come off, his captain seemed just as incapable of taking him off – yet his three wickets in the first innings, from 44 overs, cost 148 runs, more than a third of Pakistan's total.

Somerset, too, reaped the rewards of Botham's blistering bat that season: (58 of them in boundaries) in 51 minutes against Derbyshire; 47 (four sixes, four fours) off 41 balls against Kent; 66 (four sixes, eight fours) off 38 balls against Hampshire. And against Warwickshire in September, with the Test matches over, the fastest hundred of the season in 52 minutes from 56 balls. Having in the first innings hit 41 off 32 balls, he came to the wicket again with Somerset requiring 160 to win in 145 minutes: 65 minutes, 10 sixes, 12 fours and 131 runs later Botham had won the match. The very next fixture, against Worcestershire, he hit 98 (five sixes, 12 fours) off 51 balls as well as taking eight for 79 in the match. Had Ian been available throughout the season, Somerset must surely have challenged for the County Championship. As it was they had to settle for a successful defence of the Benson and Hedges Cup.

Given such outstanding form, especially with the bat, much was expected of Ian Botham when England wintered in Australia and New Zealand. Yet once again he disappointed his admirers, even though he took most wickets on the tour and with his captain Willis was the leading wicket-taker in the five-match series. When he dismissed Thomson to win the Melbourne Test for England, he became only the second Englishman, after Wilfred Rhodes, to score 1,000 runs and take 100 wickets against Australia.

At 40.50 apiece, however, his 18 Test wickets were expensive – and although he bowled most overs in the series for England, he was never fully fit. During the one-day competition at the end of the tour he was nursing a strained side, and in the Test matches it had looked sometimes as if his old back injury was troubling him. Moreover, as the tour progressed he became decidedly overweight and this, too, affected his bowling.

Not getting his left shoulder round in the delivery stride, he was bowling with an open-chested action, without rhythm or timing. His out-swinger started too early to be a surprise delivery. His bouncer looked positively friendly. Only when, on occasions, he operated off a short run did he bring to mind the match-winning swing bowler of old.

While his fielding remained brilliant, whether in his own advanced second-slip position or in the outfield, his batting was solid rather than spectacular. His top score on the tour was 65 against Western Australia and again, while opening, against New Zealand in the one-day series. It was as if, just as he had when first at Somerset, he was trying to prove himself to Australians and was trying too hard. It needed a Close or a Brearley, a strong personality, to readjust his sights and find a proper perspective. Left to himself, he looked to be in danger of destroying his talent, his image and ultimately himself.

Not one for the coaching manual, and a worry
for the purists; Ian's spectacular reverse sweep
is seen in operation against the Indians at Old
Trafford in 1982.

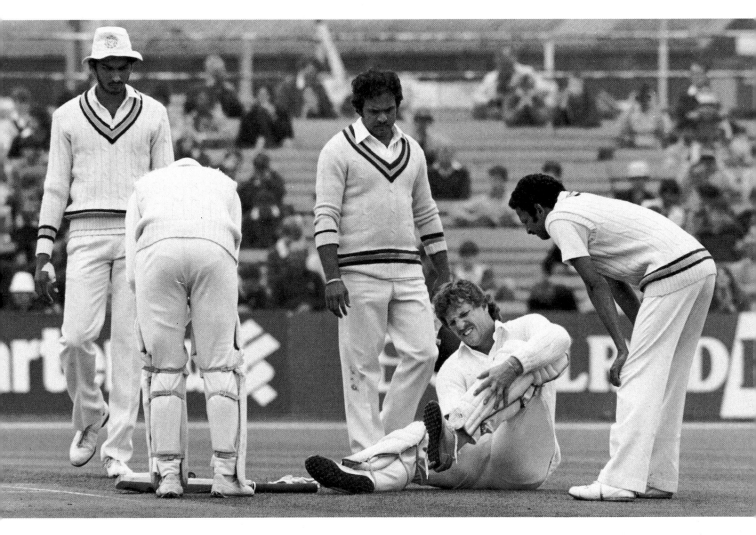

Ian removes his boot after receiving a painful blow at Old Trafford in the
second Test against India (above).

His toe was badly bruised and he batted in the following Test at The Oval
with modified footwear (right and opposite).

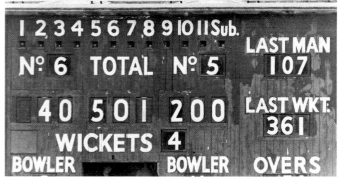

Botham and Randall together admire the scoreboard (above) as Ian makes his first Test double-century, bruised toe and reverse sweeps notwithstanding.

Somerset won the 1982 Benson and Hedges Cup final against Nottinghamshire by nine wickets. On the balcony before start of play Vic Marks (Gold Award winner), Viv Richards (51), Brian Rose (captain), Ian Botham (two for 19) and Peter Denning (22) seem to be enjoying themselves.

Sunil Gavaskar (below) gets the consolation of an autograph on his plaster-cast. He had been hit by a square cut from Ian while fielding very close during the Oval Test.

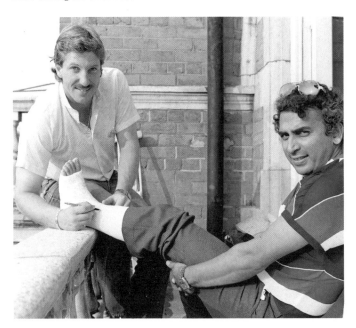

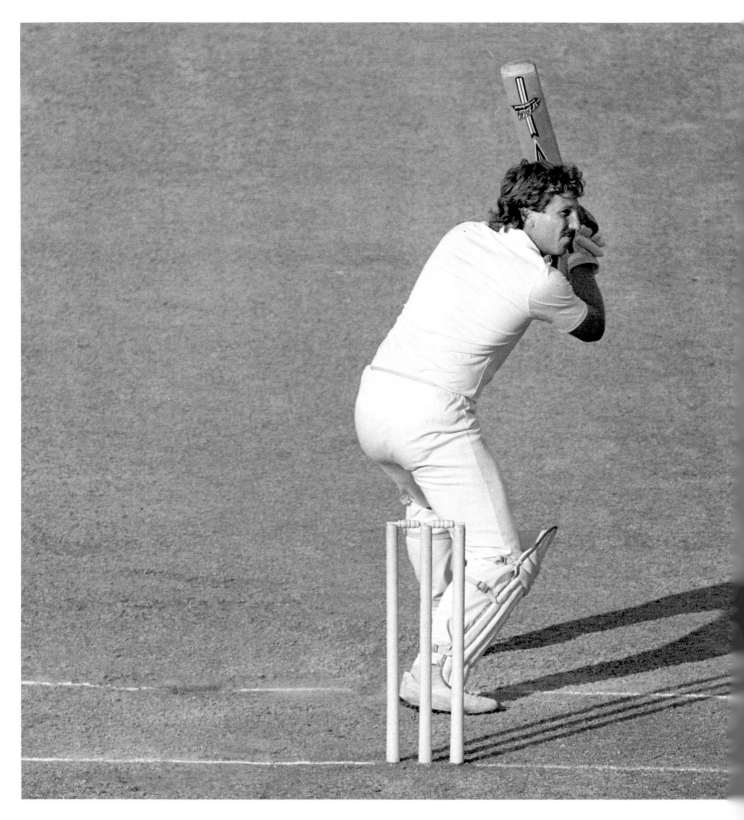

Batting in the lengthening shadows (Lord's Test v Pakistan 1982).

Ian Botham and captaincy pose one of the enigmas of English cricket in the eighties. He has so much personality – 'charisma' is the word used in a Mike Brearley analysis – that he is virtually ungovernable. But is he himself fit to govern?

Left: Botham and Willis. Was Willis any more suitable to govern? *Photograph by Jan Traylen*

Right: Gower and Botham during the Pakistan Test at Lord's (1982).

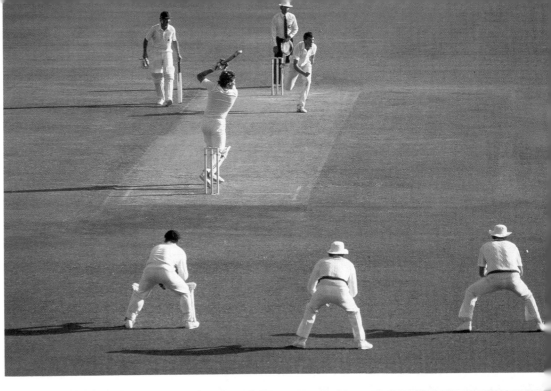

Yet another landmark in the phenomenal career of I.T.Botham; he hits his 3000th run in Test cricket off Geoff Lawson at the WACA ground in Perth during the first Test of the 1982–83 series against Australia.

Ian hooks in the second Test at Brisbane; he made 40 in the first innings.

Also at Brisbane, Ian removes Dyson's middle stump.

Touring is not all hard work, although these days the itineraries allow very few days for relaxation. From time to time there is a round of golf, a day at the beach, or perhaps a barbecue. For years one of the highlights of the Australian tour has been the rest day of the Adelaide Test – a visit to the Yalumba winery in the Barossa Valley; Ian and Dennis Lillee (above) enjoy the pool. Another Christmas Day on tour and the outrageous costumes for lunch in Melbourne include manager Doug Insole masquerading as Harvey Smith and Allan Lamb as the pink panther.

Botham's name appears in reverse from the inside of the new scoreboard at the Melbourne Cricket Ground (Boxing Day 1982). Outside it's a video show, but inside it's computers and television monitors.

A chip off the old block? Liam Botham warms up, watched by a distinguished audience.

The 1982–83 Melbourne Test resulted in a cliff-hanging finish. As the match approached its climax, Ian appeals in desperation against Hughes (far right) and attempts to run out Jeff Thomson during his final-wicket stand with Allan Border (below).

One-day cricket produces its share of thrills, spills and run-outs. In these photos of the 1983 Prudential World Cup Ian is having a mixed time.

Left: He is run out against Sri Lanka at Taunton.

Below: In spite of hitting the stumps with Mudassar some way from home, Ian didn't get the run-out. Such decisions are easy to make with a still photograph to study at leisure – much less so for the umpire in the middle at Lord's.

England lost to India in the semi-final at Old Trafford. Here Ian just makes it while Kirmani appears to be performing a balancing act on the ball.

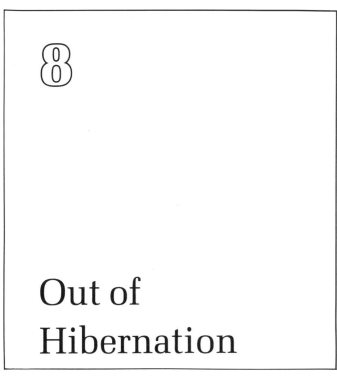

8

Out of Hibernation

In 1984, 10 years after he made his first-class début for Somerset, Ian Botham announced that he would not be available for the England team to tour India that coming winter. Instead, he wanted time to be with his family, play some football and have a rest from cricket. He had earned it. He had not, since making his début for England in 1977, spent a winter at home: and by the end of 1984 he had played in 73 Test matches, 65 of them consecutive (equalling Alan Knott's record for England), and in 72 one-day internationals.

Generally Ian's decision was welcomed. The break from cricket, it was felt, would do him good. Instances were quoted of other players who had not always gone on tour: Greg Chappell in recent years; from an earlier era, Alec Bedser, who in 10 years as an England player never toured India or the West Indies. There was never any question of these players not regaining their Test place, such was their stature, yet when England returned from India, having won the series under Gower's captaincy, the question being asked was whether Ian Botham would regain his place in the England side. This of the player who, even forgetting for a moment his 4,159 runs, 13 hundreds and 312 wickets for England, had the previous season been his country's leading wicket-taker and second-highest run-getter in the series against West Indies.

Botham's critics spoke of his destructive personality, his adverse influence on the other players, the fact that he was not easy to captain; that the team spirit in India had been happier without his overwhelming presence. What they were saying, of course, was that Botham was larger in life than those around him; which no-one could doubt. His talents, his appetite for life, are immense. It is easy to appreciate that on tour he can become easily bored, easily diverted. For Botham is a man of action, whereas tours abroad, involving so much travel, contain long periods of inaction.

The decline from headline hero to cricket's George Best began in earnest on the England tour of Fiji, New Zealand and Pakistan in 1983-84. The previous home season, 1983, had been a World Cup year: another disappointing tournament for Ian who, playing in all of England's seven games, scored 40 runs in four innings and took eight wickets for 288 from 80 overs. England's bid for a second successive final ended in the semi-finals, beaten by the eventual World Cup winners, India.

Against New Zealand, in the Test series that followed, he began quietly but finished in typically Botham style with a hundred at Trent Bridge off 99 balls, the second fifty taking 26 balls. His 103 contained three sixes and 14 fours and set up England's handsome victory after they had been 169 for five. In the second Test at Headingley, where New Zealand won their first Test in England, he had bowled so badly in the first innings that in the second innings Willis gave him the ball only when New Zealand needed two runs to win. His first delivery was hit for four.

A successive Test hundred, his 13th in all, followed when England went to New Zealand that winter. Again England were in trouble; 115 for five: and as at Trent Bridge his partner in the recovery was Derek Randall. At Trent Bridge they had put on 186 for the sixth wicket in 32 overs; at Wellington their sixth-wicket partnership was worth 232 in 201 minutes. Laurel and Hardy could not have given better entertainment. Ian's 138 off 167 balls contained two sixes and 22 fours and, coming upon his five for 59 in New Zealand's first innings, provided his fifth such match double; no-one else had done it more than twice. There should have been another century at Auckland but, on a pitch which had already produced four hundreds, Ian was run out for 70 when his partner failed to answer his call. Shades of Christchurch in 1977-78.

While England lost the series in New Zealand, media attention began to focus on the team's off-the-field activities. There were stories of broken windows in motels, abrasive and abusive behaviour in hotels and, worst of all, of drug-taking. Ian was singled out by name. The Test and County Cricket Board were quick to investigate these allegations and found that they could not be substantiated, stating that there was 'no evidence of any off-the-field behaviour which adversely affected performances on the field'.

The day after this statement, the TCCB Disciplinary Committee met to discuss a radio interview which Ian had given, contrary to his tour contract, following his early return from the Pakistan leg of the tour. During the first one-day international, at Lahore, he had aggravated the knee injury which bothered him in New Zealand, and rather than risk further damage he flew home for 'keyhole surgery'. It was while in hospital that he made a derogatory remark about Pakistan: to the effect that it was a good place to send one's mother-in-law for a holiday. Broadcast while England were still touring Pakistan, it caused considerable embarrassment, the upshot of which was a fine of £1,000, a reprimand, and a strong warning as to Ian's future conduct.

It was that warning which fired speculation about Ian's England career when a small amount of cannabis was found at his home at the end of the year and he was subsequently fined for possession of the drug. The TCCB, however, decided that no action would be taken by them, while Somerset, who had appointed Botham as their captain in 1984, confirmed that he would still lead the county in 1985.

He was quick to repay their vote of confidence. Having gone through 1984, his benefit season, without a hundred – for the first season since 1975 – in the second Championship match of 1985, against Glamorgan, he hit 100 off 76 balls, his half-century coming off 35 balls. In the previous match he had scored 90 (50 off 32 balls) and 50 against Nottinghamshire. Somerset's fourth first-class fixture was against Allan Border's Australians: and with memories of his 1977 exploits against Greg Chappell's side and the national press eager for his first clash with the tourists, Ian began with a blitz, hitting fifty off 30 balls on the first evening. But, victim of his own impetuousness, he was stumped in the third over next morning. His *tour de force* of the early summer, however, was a turbo-charged 149 off 106 balls against Hampshire – like the earlier innings, at Taunton. Ian went to the wicket with Somerset 58 for four against Malcolm Marshall and Tim Tremlett in damp, overcast conditions: his hundred came off 76 balls; altogether he hit six sixes and 20 fours. His striking of the ball was brutal.

Writing of these magnificent innings, Botham's teammate Peter Roebuck said that 'At the crease he has been a storm, a violent, rolling thunder which charges the atmosphere at every appearance. His runs have been scored, not with the flashing hits of a Jessop but with the authority of a Hammond.' So his inclusion in England's squad for the Texaco Trophy series came as no surprise. Although rarely the dominating factor in one-day internationals, he had none the less scored 1,147 runs and taken 96 wickets in these games for England. His four wickets at Old Trafford and Edgbaston and Lord's made him the first player to perform the double of 1,000 runs and 100 wickets in internationals, another Botham landmark – and England supporters waited in anticipation for the renaissance of the Botham genius to find expression in the Test series against Australia.

Botham made 61 against New Zealand at Lord's (left) – his highest Test score since the 69 against Pakistan on the same ground almost a year to the day previously.

Time for a breather (right): Edgar has been injured and Graham Dilley makes a convenient prop.

Ian turns in time to see Howarth catching him off Coney's bowling during the 1983 Headingley Test. This was the first time that New Zealand had won a Test in England.

His delight at scoring the century was scarcely concealed, as was his attitude to his many critics, especially those in the press box.

Ian hooks Hadlee (right) during his Trent Bridge 103 – his first Test hundred since the 208 against India in 1982.

Ian Botham plays golf – to a handicap of 10; Seve Ballesteros plays golf but doesn't play cricket. However a study of the position of the arms, wrists, hands and heads of these two brilliant performers is intriguing. Seve has hit a one-iron a prodigious distance (a pin-high second at Wentworth's 571-yard 17th); Ian has hit a six during his 100 against New Zealand at Trent Bridge. (A vivid personal memory as the ball splintered the top of the Cornhill board three inches from my lens and richocheted into the wall immediately below the press box behind me. Ian later joked somewhat blackly that he was aiming not at me but at the press box window above.).

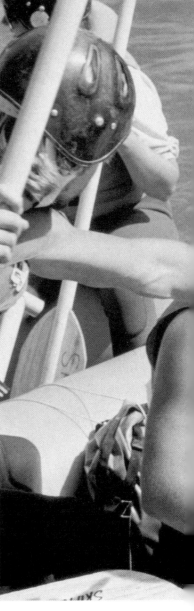

The winter tour of 1983-84 was a mixed one for Botham. Success on the field, controversy off it and finally an early return home following the New Zealand section.

The photographs (this page and overleaf) show Ian with Allan Lamb, David Gower, Graeme Fowler and Chris Smith white-water rafting on the Kawarau river near Queenstown in New Zealand's South Island.

Ian's 4000th Test run came during the 2nd Test v West Indies at Lord's in 1984 (left).

At Edgbaston in the first Test he forced umpire Meyer into evasive action with a powerful straight drive off Garner (right).

Overleaf: The Lord's pavilion forms a back-drop for Botham's hook off Baptiste during the 2nd Test in 1984.

Ian takes a brilliant catch at second slip to dismiss Larry Gomes off Richard Ellison (above) during the final Test against the West Indies at the Oval in 1984.

Viv Richards has been caught by Allott and Ian Botham is as ecstatic as ever – for him this is the most important West Indian wicket, if not the most important wicket in cricket.

Ian bowling during the spell in which he took his 300th Test wicket (left). His victim (above) was Geoffrey Dujon, who was caught by Chris Tavare at slip (5th Test v West Indies at The Oval 1984).

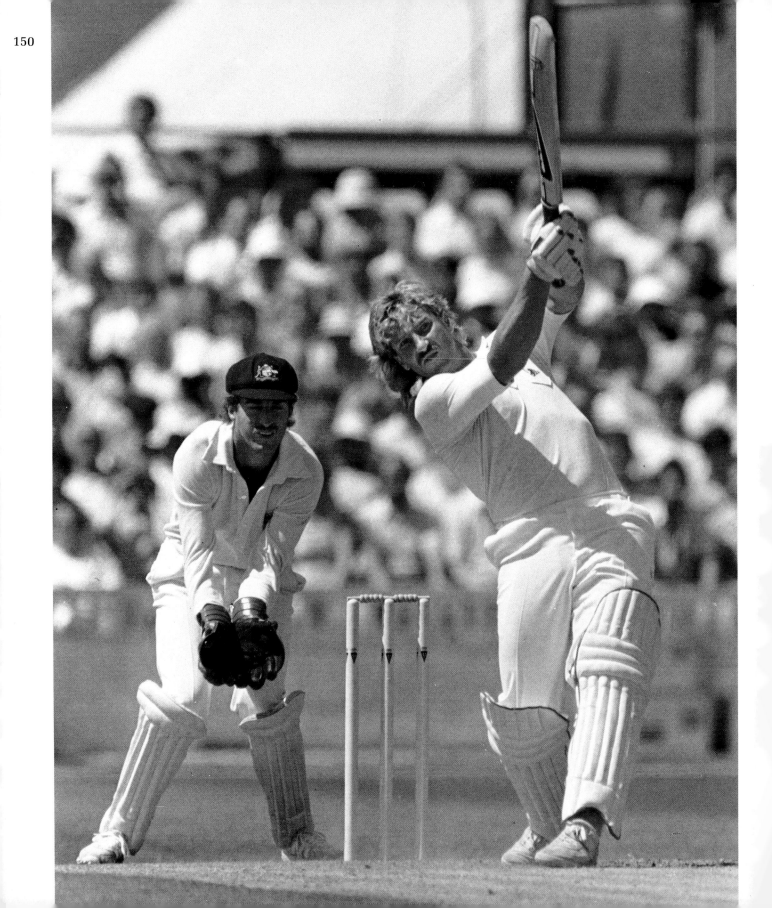

Ian sparkled in the first battle with the 1985 Australians. He produced a brilliant display at Old Trafford, including this straight six off Matthews (left).

He came to grief (right and below) while attempting a controversial reverse sweep off the same bowler. He had made 72.

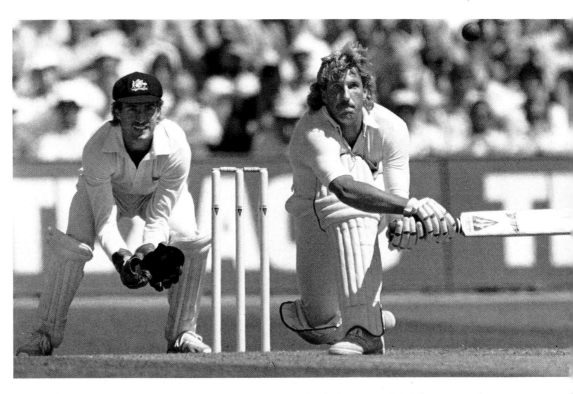

The match at Lord's produced Ian's 100th one-day international wicket (Ritchie – caught by Gooch – above); he thus became the first player to achieve the "double" in these matches. Below: setting the field with David Gower.

His repertoire included this remarkable stroke at Edgbaston (right) which sent the ball back over the bowler's head.

FIRST-CLASS CAREER SUMMARY

Season	M	I	NO	HS	Runs	Avge	100	50	Ct	St		O	R	W	Avge	BB	5w	10w
1974	18	29	3	59	441	16.96	-	1	15	-		291	739	30	24.63	5-59	1	-
1975	22	36	4	65	584	18.25	-	2	18	-		605³	1704	62	27.48	5-69	1	-
1976	20	35	5	167*	1022	34.06	1	6	16	-		563⁴	1880	66	28.48	6-16	4	1
1977	17	27	3	114	738	30.75	1	5	15	-		665⁵	1983	88	22.53	6-50	6	1
1977-78 (P)	3	2	1	22*	22	22.00	-	-	2	-		41†	153	4	38.25	2-31	-	-
(NZ)	6	10	3	126*	375	53.57	2	1	5	-		169⁴†	538	31	17.35	7-58	3	1
1978	17	20	-	108	538	26.90	2	1	11	-		605²	1640	100	16.40	8-34	10	1
1978-79 (A)	9	14	-	74	361	25.78	-	3	14	-		239³†	848	44	19.27	5-51	2	-
1979	15	20	1	137	731	38.47	2	1	21	-		436⁴	1318	46	28.65	6-81	3	-
1979-80 (A)	5	9	1	119*	217	27.12	1	-	5	-		193¹	426	21	20.28	6-78	2	1
(I)	1	1	-	114	114	114.00	1	-	-	-		48⁵	106	13	8.15	7-48	2	1
1980	18	27	-	228	1149	42.55	2	6	24	-		453³	1387	40	34.67	4-38	-	-
1980-81 (WI)	8	14	-	40	197	14.07	-	-	8	-		224²	790	23	34.34	4-77	-	-
1981	16	24	2	149*	925	42.04	3	4	19	-		574²	1712	67	25.55	6-90	4	1
1981-82 (I)	10	14	1	142	747	57.46	2	5	7	-		292³	863	22	39.22	5-61	1	-
(SL)	1	1	-	13	13	13.00	-	-	-	-		24⁵	65	3	21.66	3-28	-	-
1982	17	29	1	208	1241	44.32	3	7	7	-		491⁴	1517	66	22.98	5-46	4	-
1982-83 (A)	9	18	-	65	434	24.11	-	2	17	-		319⁴	1033	29	35.62	4-43	-	-
1983	14	21	-	152	852	40.57	3	2	10	-		232²	728	22	33.09	5-38	1	-
1983-84 (NZ)	6	8	-	138	377	47.12	1	2	4	-		163⁵	499	14	35.64	5-59	1	-
(P)	1	2	-	23	32	16.00	-	-	4	-		30	90	2	45.00	2-90	-	-
1984	17	26	1	90	797	31.88	-	7	7	-		449⁴	1562	59	26.47	8-103	4	-
TOTALS	250	387	26	(228)	11907	32.98	24	55	229	-	(43599 balls)	449.7† / 16666.4	21581	852	25.32	(8-34)	49	7

A - Australia   I - India   NZ - New Zealand   P - Pakistan   SL - Sri Lanka   W - West Indies

Teams	M	I	NO	HS	Runs	Avge	100	50	Ct	St		O	R	W	Avge	BB	5w	10w
SOMERSET	147	226	17	228	6602	31.58	9	32	116	-		3785⁴	11488	454	25.30	7-61	21	2
ENGLAND in UK	40	63	1	208	2301	37.11	8	9	41	-		1481²	4446	178	24.97	8-34	16	2
MCC in UK	4	5	2	53*	115	38.33	-	1	6	-		102³	236	14	16.85	5-43	1	-
UK TOTALS	191	294	20	(228)	9018	32.91	17	42	163	-		5369³	16170	646	25.03	(8-34)	38	4
In AUSTRALIA	23	41	1	119*	1012	25.30	1	5	36	-		239.3† / 512.5	2307	94	24.54	6-78	4	1
In INDIA	11	15	1	142	861	61.50	3	5	7	-		341.2	969	35	27.68	7-48	3	1
In NEW ZEALAND	12	18	3	138	752	50.13	3	3	9	-		169.4† / 163.5	1037	45	23.04	7-58	4	1
In PAKISTAN	4	4	1	23	54	18.00	-	-	6	-		41† / 30	243	6	40.50	2-31	-	-
In SRI LANKA	1	1	-	13	13	13.00	-	-	-	-		24⁵	65	3	21.66	3-28	-	-
In WEST INDIES	8	14	-	40	197	14.07	-	-	8	-		224²	790	23	34.34	4-77	-	-
OVERSEAS TOTALS	59	93	6	(142)	2889	33.20	7	13	66	-		449.7† / 1297.1	5411	206	26.26	(7-48)	11	3

HIGHEST SCORE: 228 Somerset v Gloucestershire at Taunton 1980.   * not out   † 8-ball overs

BEST BOWLING - INNINGS: 8-34 England v Pakistan at Lord's 1978. BB-MATCH: 13-106 England v India at Bombay 1979-80.

155

TEST MATCH CAREER SUMMARY

Season	V	M	I	NO	HS	Runs	Avge	100	50	Ct	St		O	R	W	Avge	BB	5w	10w
1977	A	2	2	-	25	25	12.50	-	-	1	-		73	202	10	20.20	5-21	2	-
1977-78	NZ	3	5	1	103	212	53.00	1	1	5	-		101†	311	17	18.29	5-73	2	-
1978	P	3	3	-	108	212	70.66	2	-	4	-		75.5	209	13	16.07	8-34	1	-
1978	NZ	3	3	-	22	51	17.00	-	-	2	-		142.1	337	24	14.04	6-34	3	1
1978-79	A	6	10	-	74	291	29.10	-	2	11	-		158.4†	567	23	24.65	4-42	-	-
1979	I	4	5	-	137	244	48.80	1	-	10	-		179	472	20	23.60	5-35	2	-
1979-80	A	3	6	1	119*	187	37.40	1	-	3	-		173.1	371	19	19.52	6-78	2	1
1979-80	I	1	1	-	114	114	114.00	1	-	-	-		48.5	106	13	8.15	7-48	2	1
1980	WI	5	9	-	57	169	18.77	-	1	2	-		131	385	13	29.61	3-50	-	-
1980	A	1	1	-	0	0	0.00	-	-	-	-		31.2	132	1	132.00	1-43	-	-
1980-81	WI	4	7	-	26	73	10.42	-	-	5	-		145.2	492	15	32.80	4-77	-	-
1981	A	6	12	1	149*	399	36.27	2	1	12	-		272.3	700	34	20.58	6-95	3	1
1981-82	I	6	8	-	142	440	55.00	1	4	3	-		240.3	660	17	38.82	5-61	1	-
1981-82	SL	1	1	-	13	13	13.00	-	-	-	-		24.5	65	3	21.66	3-28	-	-
1982	I	3	3	-	208	403	134.33	2	1	1	-		93.3	320	9	35.55	5-46	1	-
1982	P	3	6	-	69	163	27.16	-	2	-	-		150.5	478	18	26.55	5-74	1	-
1982-83	A	5	10	-	58	270	27.00	-	1	9	-		213.5	729	18	40.50	4-75	-	-
1983	NZ	4	8	-	103	282	35.25	1	1	3	-		112.5	340	10	34.00	4-50	-	-
1983-84	NZ	3	4	-	138	226	56.50	1	1	3	-		109.4	354	7	50.57	5-59	1	-
1983-84	P	1	2	-	22	32	16.00	-	-	4	-		30	90	2	45.00	2-90	-	-
1984	WI	5	10	-	81	347	34.70	-	3	5	-		163.2	667	19	35.10	8-103	2	-
1984	SL	1	1	-	6	6	6.00	-	-	-	-		56	204	7	29.14	6-90	1	-
TOTALS		73	117	3	(208)	4159	36.48	13	18	84	-	16881 balls { 259.4† 2467.3		8191	312	26.25	(8-34)	24	4

Opponents	M	I	NO	HS	Runs	Avge	100	50	Ct	St		O	R	W	Avge	BB	5w	10w
AUSTRALIA	23	41	2	149*	1172	30.05	3	4	36	-	{158.4† 763.5	2701	105	25.72	6-78	7	2
WEST INDIES	14	26	-	81	589	22.65	-	4	12	-	439.4	1544	47	32.85	8-103	2	-
NEW ZEALAND	13	20	1	138	771	40.57	3	3	13	-	{101† 364.4	1342	58	23.13	6-34	6	1
INDIA	14	17	-	208	1201	70.64	5	5	14	-	561.5	1558	59	26.40	7-48	6	1
PAKISTAN	7	11	-	108	407	37.00	2	2	9	-	256.4	777	33	23.54	8-34	2	-
SRI LANKA	2	2	-	13	19	9.50	-	-	-	-	80.5	269	10	26.90	6-90	1	-
TOTALS	73	117	3	(208)	4159	36.48	13	18	84	-	{259.4† 2467.3	8191	312	26.25	(8-34)	24	4

Venues	M	I	NO	HS	Runs	Avge	100	50	Ct	St		O	R	W	Avge	BB	5w	10w
AT HOME	40	63	1	208	2301	37.11	8	9	41	-	1481.2	4446	178	24.97	8-34	16	2
OVERSEAS	33	54	2	142	1858	35.73	5	9	43	-	{259.4† 986.1	3745	134	27.94	7-48	8	2

* not out   † 8-ball overs

IAN BOTHAM'S 149 NOT OUT AT HEADINGLEY

KIRKSTALL LANE END

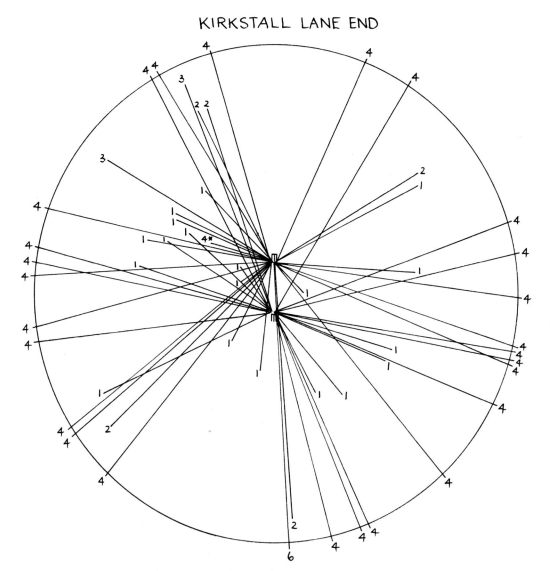

MAIN STAND END

Runs	Balls	Minutes	6s	4s
50	57	110	-	8
100	87	155	1	19
149	148	219	1	27

Bowler	Balls	Runs	6s	4s
ALDERMAN	62	68	1	11
BRIGHT	21	15	-	3
LAWSON	44	44	-	8
LILLEE	21	22	-	5

BOTHAM'S SCORING SEQUENCE

0002042000040100001000410000031
0013014204*00100040400000404044400
444104000000640100040 4 [†] 400010201
0001000100010040001000401042041 00
40100044100040000000.

* 4 overthrows to the mid-wicket boundary
† off a no-ball

© BILL FRINDALL 1981

LIMITED-OVERS INTERNATIONALS CAREER SUMMARY

Competition	M	I	NO	HS	Runs	Avge	100	50	Ct	St		Balls	R	W	Avge	BB	5w	Runs/ 100 balls
PT/TT	20	19	3	49	312	19.50	-	-	8	-		1114	787	27	29.14	4-56	-	70.6
PC	12	8	1	22	105	15.00	-	-	6	-		798	456	14	32.57	2-12	-	57.1
BHWS	19	18	-	65	319	17.72	-	1	5	-		902	654	29	22.55	3-29	-	72.5
OTHERS	21	19	4	60	411	27.40	-	3	6	-		948	636	26	24.46	3-16	-	67.1
TOTALS	72	64	8	(65)	1147	20.48	-	4	25	-		3762	2533	96	26.38	(4-56)	-	67.3

PT - Prudential Trophy. TT - Texaco Trophy. PC - Prudential Cup. BHWS - Benson & Hedges World Series.

Figures do not include 1985 season.

Index